Dyslexia and
Physical Education

Other titles in this series

Introduction to Dyslexia
Lindsay Peer and Gavin Reid
1-85346-964-5

Dyslexia and Design & Technology
Frances Ranaldi
1-84312-015-1

Dyslexia and Drama
Helen Eadon
1-84312-048-8

Dyslexia and English
Elizabeth Turner and Jayne Pughe
1-85346-967-X

Dyslexia and Foreign Language Learning
Gaining Success in an Inclusive Context
Margaret Crombie and Elke Schneider
1-85346-966-1

Dyslexia and General Science
Stephen Wyatt
1-84312-050-X

Dyslexia and History
Richard Dargie
1-84312-014-3

Dyslexia and Maths
Julie Kay and Dorian Yeo
1-85346-965-3

Dyslexia and Music
Jane Kirk
1-84312-047-X

Dyslexia and Physical Education

Madeleine Portwood

David Fulton Publishers

London

David Fulton Publishers Ltd
The Chiswick Centre, 414 Chiswick High Road, London W4 5TF

www.fultonpublishers.co.uk

David Fulton Publishers is a division of Granada Learning Limited,
part of Granada plc.

First published 2003

10 9 8 7 6 5 4 3 2 1

British Library Cataloguing in Publication Data
A Catalogue record for this book is available from the British
Library.

ISBN 1 85346 970 X

Typeset by Pracharak Technologies (P) Ltd, Madras, India
Printed and bound in Great Britain by Ashford Colour Press Ltd,
Gosport, Hants.

Contents

Acknowledgements

I would like to extend my thanks to the children and parents who have contributed to this book in allowing their photographs and case studies to be presented, particularly the pupils of Montalbo Primary School.

I have benefited from the support of my professional colleagues who, through their particular specialisms and involvement with youngsters, have supplied invaluable supplementary material:

- Shaun Myers, Ingleton Primary School, who has provided much of the inspiration for the suggested activities;

- Alan Duff, Advisor in Physical Education and Chris Ridley, Motor Skills Project Coordinator;

- Master David Jordinson and members of the Chungdokwan Taekwondo Organisation.

Additionally, I thank the following students who gave their time to meet with me personally: Adam, Ben, Callum, Claire, Craig, Gary, Hannah, Jack, Jamie, Kiel, Lee, Luke, Nicholas, Sammy and Toni.

Finally, I thank those who have been directly involved in the production of this text:

- John Portwood (IT support)

- Mike Campos (photography)

Foreword

We are indeed privileged to be asked to write a foreword for this much-needed book on dyslexia and physical education by Madeleine Portwood. Madeleine is well-equipped to write such a book and her experience in the field, both in research and practice, comes through very clearly.

As Madeleine Portwood claims, Physical Education is a crucial area for developing motor and coordination skills and an area that is sometimes neglected in relation to its value in developing cognitive and other learning skills needed by all children to perform in all areas of the curriculum. This, of course, as Madeleine suggests, is of greater importance for children with dyslexia. This is particularly pertinent as the research highlights the co-occurrence between dyslexia and other difficulties such as Developmental Coordination Disorders (DCD) and Attention Deficit (Hyperactivity) Disorders (ADHD), as well as other difficulties such as spatial awareness, rhythm, timing and visual processing. This concept of co-occurrence highlights the responsibility of all involved in crucial subject areas such as physical education. It emphasises the need to recognise the nature of the difficulties experienced by many children with dyslexia and to appreciate the role intervention can play, not only in their own subject, but also across the whole curriculum and its influence on the child's cognitive development.

Madeleine Portwood emphasises this by discussing the importance of early development, and the information presented in these chapters – such as the movement checklist and the examples of activities that can help in the development of motor skills – will be invaluable to those less experienced in the early stages such as teachers in secondary schools.

One of the strengths of this book is that the author has ensured that it will meet the needs of PE specialists across all stages. The chapters on the development of movement skills are relevant throughout all stages. Additionally, the book also offers a chapter dedicated to secondary education which can, in fact, be a neglected area in relation to its importance in the child's overall academic performance. As the author points out, PE is a subject that is often 'squeezed out' by other curriculum demands. This is a situation that must be reversed, and it is hoped that this book will highlight the importance of PE for children with dyslexia. She points out in the conclusion of this book that programmes and activities focusing on the development of motor skills can have a significant effect on the acquisition of reading skills and on concentration.

We, as editors of this series of books on dyslexia and different subject areas, are delighted to recommend this book to schools and encourage every school in the country to obtain it. Not only will this serve the needs of PE specialists, many of whom are desperately seeking information of this kind, but also the needs of children with dyslexia across the whole spectrum of learning and literacy.

Lindsay Peer CBE
Gavin Reid
June 2003

Introduction

When I was approached by Lindsay Peer and Gavin Reid to write a book entitled *Dyslexia and Physical Education*, the title suggested, I thought, that the relationship between the two was problematic. Was this necessarily the case? I remembered seeing large posters produced by the British Dyslexia Association (BDA) displaying the faces of Duncan Goodhew, Sir Steve Redgrave and Sir Jackie Stewart (to name but a few), all famous sportsmen who are dyslexic. A number of questions required answers:

- What proportion of dyslexic individuals experience difficulties with coordination and movement?
- How can they best be supported?
- How can we ensure that those with great potential are able to achieve?

The aim of this book is to review published research linking dyslexia and the development of physical skills, and on the basis of these findings, to identify models of good practice which promote learning. I am writing for parents and teachers, and in the following chapters I will discuss the importance of physical education from birth to adolescence. It is important to examine not only the development of coordinated movement but also the implications, socially and emotionally, for children who struggle to acquire these skills.

Physical Education is often the subject that is 'squeezed out' as a result of other demands within the National Curriculum. It may also be, in part, because many teachers, particularly in primary education, are anxious about their own skill base in this subject.

I have included suggestions for non-specialist teachers to enable them to provide high-quality learning experiences through Physical Education which will help students with dyslexia and support others in the class with coordination difficulties. The recommended activities can be integrated with other recognised schemes such as the

'Top Start' programme or the units of work prepared by the DfES for PE in KS1, 2 and 3. What is essential is that the skills taught relate directly to the neurological and physiological competence of the child.

The first chapter provides an overview of current research and sets the context for the rest of the book. Activities for pre-school and nursery-age children are discussed separately.

As there are wide-ranging abilities of children within the same key stage, it seemed appropriate to divide the next chapters into skill development rather than by pupil age. They present graded activities, which develop sequentially. The headings are:

- Balance.

- Movement.

- Coordination.

This enables the programmes to be accessed by children of any age where the entry point is determined by their current skill level.

On transfer to secondary education, the pupils are provided with a range of opportunities to focus more specifically on areas of skill, and this forms the discussion in the next chapter.

Many of the suggested activities are school-based, but they can easily be adapted for use elsewhere: the youth club; the sports centre, at home.

For some youngsters the school environment overwhelms them with feelings of failure. For them the answer may well lie elsewhere. The final chapter is given to a discussion of the influence of martial arts in relation to children and young adults with specific learning difficulties. It dispels the myth that only well-coordinated, aggressive individuals should 'apply'. As a discipline it is supportive of those individuals who require time to acquire new skills. Case studies highlight the fundamental requirement to achieve goals, which must be self-determined.

Chapter 1

An Overview of Research

Dyslexia is best described as a combination of abilities and difficulties that affect the learning process in one or more of reading, spelling and writing. Accompanying weaknesses may be identified in areas of speed of visual processing, short-term memory, sequencing and organisation, auditory and/ or visual perception, spoken language and motor skills. It is particularly related to mastering and using written language, which may include alphabetic, numeric and musical notation. (Peer 2003)

Substantive research into the connection between dyslexia and deficits in motor skills was published in Duffy and Geschwind (1985). Observational assessment suggested that dyslexic children showed impaired development in a series of motor tasks relating to speed of movement, balance and coordination, and acquiring new skills was very difficult (Denckla *et al.* 1985). The tasks included foot-tapping, heel-toe placement, finger sequencing and copying. Rudel (1985) described these findings as a 'maturational lag', which would improve with age.

The development of 'new' skills was the focus of much research undertaken by Fawcett and Nicolson in the early 1990s, particularly the automaticity of motor development, the point at which a skill is learned and can be completed virtually without thought. They discovered that children with dyslexia put more effort into 'planning' sequential movements when compared with 'controls' matched for age and ability. Nicolson and Fawcett (1990) assessed the performance of 23 thirteen-year-old dyslexic children using a series of motor tasks. A beam was constructed, using large building blocks, six inches high, five inches wide and eight feet in length. Initially, the tasks set were:

- balancing, one foot on the floor, arms outstretched, for one minute;

- balancing, one foot on the beam, leg straight, arms outstretched, for one minute;

- balancing on the beam on one leg, with bent knee, for 30 seconds;

- balancing on the beam on one leg, with bent knee, for one minute; and

- walking along the beam, with arms outstretched.

Error points for incorrect foot position, wobble, overbalancing and stepping off the beam were recorded.

A secondary task was then introduced and the children were asked to count or press a button.

The results of the dyslexic children were compared with a group of matched controls. Under the first conditions, 'just balancing', the dyslexic children achieved as well as the controls. However, when 'dual' tasks were undertaken, the dyslexic children's performance deteriorated significantly, unlike that of the controls.

Wolff *et al.* (1990) provided further evidence in experiments that identified motor difficulties in fine, repetitive finger and hand movements in dyslexic children, when bimanual coordination is required, but not when comparing performance on single-handed activities. Wolff interprets the results not just as the inability to coordinate and move each finger quickly, but an indication of a deficit in general ability to rapidly coordinate asynchronous and asymmetric movement.

Furthermore, Wolff discovered motor deficits in adults as well as children with dyslexia in both bimanual alternation and asynchronous coordination. This suggests that coordination difficulties do not necessarily disappear with maturation, as reported by Rudel (1985).

Further evidence indicating that children with dyslexia have 'persistent and unexpectedly severe problems in skill' is presented in further research by Fawcett and Nicolson (1995). The study comprised groups of children with dyslexia and matched controls using two tests of motor skill (bead threading and peg moving) and one test of articulatory skill (speed of articulating well-known words). The effect of maturation was monitored by using three age groups: 8, 13 and 17 years.

Bead threading

The children were given a basket containing round wooden beads and instructed to take them one at a time and thread them on the string as quickly as possible for a period of one minute.

Pegboard

The top row of the board was fitted with pegs and the child was instructed to move the pegs one at a time into the third row (missing the second). On completing the row, the children moved the pegs again two rows down the board and this was repeated five times. The mean of the trials was calculated.

Articulation Rate

The children were asked to say the words 'bus', 'monkey' and 'butterfly' several times as quickly as possible. The time taken for five repetitions of each word was measured to the nearest centisecond.

Results

The performance of children with dyslexia was consistently below that of their matched controls in every outcome measure. Depending on the task, between 40 per cent and 100 per cent of the dyslexic children in the study had a performance more than one standard deviation below that of the same-age control group. The youngest dyslexic children resorted to using both hands, swapping between left and right when completing the pegboard. They had similar problems with the bead-threading task.

When articulating the three-syllable word 'butterfly', the dyslexic children in all three age groups had difficulties and muddled the sound sequences.

Although there is evidence of improvement with age in the groups of dyslexic children, the controls reached the ceiling of the assessments by age 13. Fawcett and Nicolson (1995) conclude that 'motor skill and articulation deficits persist into adolescence'.

To provide further evidence to support the idea that children and adults with dyslexia show signs of delayed automaticity of motor development and have difficulty processing sound sequences, Fawcett and Nicolson (1999) completed an additional series of experimental tasks involving 126 dyslexic and control children. The assessment included measurement of:

Postural stability: subjects were asked to stand up straight, feet together and arms at their sides, and were pushed in the lower back. The pushing was performed using the balance tester developed by Fawcett and Nicolson (1996). The score was determined by the degree of movement from non-sway stepping forward to complete loss of balance.

Arm shake: the examiner grips the wrist of the subject and shakes it gently, side to side. A score for 'movement', i.e. very floppy, shows evidence of poor muscle tone.

Toe tapping: subjects were required to tap their feet ten times as quickly as possible.

The results indicated that more than 95 per cent of dyslexic children showed evidence of deficits in postural stability and muscle tone. It was also noted that the degree of deficit was comparable in magnitude to the children's reading and spelling deficits.

Wolff (1999) also links impaired motor skills with language delay. In his study of dyslexic children, 90 per cent of those with motor coordination deficits also had motor speech deficits measured by a task involving repetitive syllable production. He concludes: 'the detailed analysis of co-articulation in speech production may be one pathway by which impaired timing precision in motor action impinges on reading and writing deficits in developmental dyslexia'.

There is supportive evidence to link motor deficits and dyslexia. Ramus *et al.* (2003), reporting on a study into motor control and phonology in dyslexic children, suggest that part of the discrepancy in motor skills is due to dyslexic individuals who had additional disorders: ADHD and DCD (dyspraxia).

The purpose of this study was to attempt to replicate the findings of Fawcett and Nicolson: that dyslexic children are impaired on a range of tasks involving manual dexterity, balance and coordination, and that motor dysfunction might be the cause of dyslexia.

Wimmer *et al.* (1998) suggested that the presence of ADHD in any study sample of dyslexic children would account for the variance in the percentage of individuals identified with coordination difficulties.

Kaplan *et al.* (1998) reported that 63 per cent of the dyslexic children in their study also had DCD (dyspraxia).

My own research (Portwood 1999, 2000), involving more than 600 school-aged children with dyspraxia, indicated that there was a co-occurrence with dyslexia in more than 50 per cent of those studied. It seems probable that in selecting a population sample on the basis of one set of criteria, e.g. factors associated with dyslexia, there will be evidence of other co-occurring neurodevelopmental disorders.

Another study by Ramus *et al.* (2003) focused on a group of dyslexic 8–12-year-old children with matched controls. Assessment of motor control and phonological skills was undertaken. Twenty-two children were selected, and those with co-occurring ADHD and DCD were actively sought, together with 'pure' dyslexics. Of the 22 dyslexic participants, seven were also diagnosed with ADHD, one with DCD and two with both ADHD and DCD. The same number of children, matched for age and ability, were recruited from a mainstream school to act as controls.

The Phonological Assessment Battery (Frederickson *et al.* 1997) was administered. The tests included: alliteration, rhyme, naming speed (pictures and digits), spoonerisms and a range of fluency assessments. The four motor tests devised by Nicolson and Fawcett for use in their own studies were: finger to thumb sequencing; bead threading, postural stability; and tone estimation (two tones presented successively with the requirement to say which of the two is longer).

Results

In the motor assessment, three children in the dyslexic group could not attempt the finger/thumb task. Of the three, one was dyslexic with ADHD, one was dyslexic with DCD, and the other was dyslexic, ADHD and DCD. In the study, twelve children were identified with 'pure' dyslexia and ten with co-occurring presentations. In total, five pure dyslexic children (42 per cent) and eight with co-occurrence (80 per cent) were poorer than controls in motor tasks. This provides additional evidence to support the idea that in the 'pure dyslexic' population there are problems with motor control, although not in every case. However, the results from this study suggest that co-occurrence of other neurodevelopmental disorders with dyslexia increases the likelihood of more severe impairment.

Compounding the motor difficulty identified in the majority of dyslexic children, there are additional factors, such as poor auditory sequencing, deficits in detecting movement and problems with binocular convergence (Eden *et al.* 1996;, Stein and Glickstein 1992). Studies of perceptual skills suggest that dyslexic subjects process visual information more slowly than controls. These visual impairments were found in more than 75 per cent of the dyslexic children assessed (Livingstone *et al.* 1991).

The problems with visual processing associated with dyslexia include spatial awareness, timing and rhythm (Fawcett and Nicolson 1992, 1999). This, in turn, has a direct effect on skills such as catching a ball or simply maintaining orientation for balance (Willows *et al.* 1993).

Any programme of activities to promote the development of motor skills should therefore include:

- opportunities to practise visual sequencing with specified time constraints;

- activities to develop binocular coordination using near and distant targets;

- opportunities to sequence sound and movement; and

- exercises which specifically integrate sensory information, i.e. movement in response to visual and auditory stimuli.

Chapter 2

Physical Development in the Early Years

The media are constantly raising awareness of rising levels of obesity in children and its probable long-term effect on future wellbeing – the outcomes of a restricted diet and limited exercise are evident. There are also increasing numbers of children identified with specific learning difficulties: dyslexia, dyspraxia and Attention Deficit Hyperactivity Disorder (ADHD). At the same time there is a rise in the incidence of allergies, such as asthma and hay fever. Parents are concerned about lack of concentration in their children, and teachers describe far higher levels of excitability in their pupils.

Many of these developments must be attributed to lifestyle changes. Diet is one factor, but perhaps less obvious is the effect of delayed development of motor skills on future learning outcomes. 'Movement is a child's first language – it is the first medium of expansion of the physical and emotional conditions of an individual. Self control begins with the control of movement' (Kiphard and Schilling 1994).

External influences affect opportunities for motor development. Although some adults now make determined attempts to attend regular sessions in the gym, children spend much less time engaged in physical activities than they did 20 years ago. Preferred pastimes revolve around computers and television screens, where children's programmes are on offer round the clock. Sometimes, even with the best of intentions, children's opportunities to develop early motor skills are restricted.

There are concerns among health professionals that in a significant number of children the crawling stage is delayed or even omitted. In my own research (Portwood 1999), 82 per cent of the 600 children identified with dyspraxia/dyslexia failed to crawl, preferring to bottom-shuffle instead. Some theorists suggest that this may relate to concerns regarding 'cot death syndrome' causing parents to place babies on their backs to sleep. This makes rolling more difficult, and a child must be able to lie face down to achieve a four-point kneeling position – a prerequisite for crawling.

Baby-walkers also have a detrimental effect on the development of skills. They discourage crawling because they facilitate much faster motor movement than the children could achieve for themselves. They also encourage the child to 'toe-walk' rather than use the whole of the foot.

The outcome of research undertaken by Goddard and Hyland (1998) found that there were significant differences in the early development of groups of seven- and eight-year-old children who had reading, writing and copying difficulties when compared with matched controls. The children in the first groups had a 'cluster' of factors in early development relating to balance, motor skills and auditory processing. They were learning to walk later (16+ months), and many did not crawl. They were late talking, riding a bike and catching a ball, and they struggled to complete fine motor tasks: doing up buttons and tying shoelaces. The discrepancy between the two groups increased over time as delays in early motor development continued to impact upon learning, which was dependent upon the motor system for expression, reading, writing and copying.

Developing early movement skills

There are a series of developmental stages through which the child should progress. Initially, the child learns to move his/her eyes and to track objects. This is followed by an attempt at reaching and grasping. Through trial and error the child learns about judging speed, distance and the position of their hands in space. The brain then stores this information and eventually the 'planning' of the movement becomes instinctive and reflexive, described in Nicolson and Fawcett (1990) as the 'automatisation of skills'. It is important for the child to develop these skills sequentially and the goal is to achieve coordination and control of balance and motor skills.

The parent/carer should provide the child with opportunities to extend their skills, and that may require the introduction of structured activities without which their development would be left to chance. Responding to concerns in relation to increasing numbers of children identified in nursery as having coordination difficulties, Wetton (1997) said, 'We can no longer leave this learning to the osmosis approach in which children select their own play and, as a consequence, their own learning.'

The developmental stages before a child is able to stand and balance independently are crucial. Children who have poorly developed postural control find it difficult to sit still and focus their attention. They fidget constantly and engage in a range of associated movements – classic signs of ADHD. Skills are not 'automatic' and the brain struggles to maintain control over balance, posture and involuntary movements (Kohen-Raz 1986). Expected developmental progress is as follows:

Movement checklist

0–12 months:

- turns head from side to side when placed on front or back;
- visually tracks object from side to side;
- when placed on back, makes random movements with arms and legs;
- when placed on front, raises head and then chest from floor;
- makes purposeful movements towards object secured in line of vision;
- brings hands together in mid-line;
- fingers extended from grasping reflex;
- when placed on front, is able to press down with hands and raise chest from floor;
- attempts to roll from side to side;
- in supported sitting position, is able to rotate head and upper body;
- reaches and grasps objects with hands;
- rolls from front to back and reverse;
- places foot (flat) on floor and 'stands' with total adult support;
- sits unsupported (shows saving reflexes);

- pivots in sitting position and moves freely to knees;
- crawls on all fours;
- holds upright kneeling;
- pushes from kneeling to standing position with support;
- still standing with support, transfers weight between feet;
- begins to cruise round the furniture;
- walks with adult support, both hands held or pushing toy;
- moves from a standing to sitting position.

12–24 months:

- stands independently, leaning against adult or furniture;
- picks up small objects, fingers and thumb in opposition;
- removes objects from pegboard or handled inset puzzle;
- walks with one hand held;
- sits on floor (legs 'V' shaped) and rolls ball away from self;
- takes a few independent steps;
- stands alone;
- crawls up stairs;
- places one two-inch block on top of another;
- makes 'scribble' marks on paper;
- develops hand preference;
- makes marks on paper of same direction (across, up, down);
- completes single-piece form board;
- separates screw toys;
- bends over to pick up objects without falling over;
- copies circular scribble;
- throws a ball;

- uses preferred hand most of the time;

- walks backwards safely.

In the early years, the child develops balance skills coordinating all parts of the body through a process of trial and error. There is also a developing awareness of speed and distance. Initially, a child making his first independent steps realises that without support the only means of maintaining upright balance is to move off at speed. When the motion decreases, balance has greater dependency upon postural control. The young child is unable to use his limbs to counterbalance the body effectively.

Research presented in Chapter 1 suggests that many dyslexic children experience delays in the acquisition of new skills and they require repeated opportunities to practise them. It is unlikely that they will be developed naturally, so adult involvement is necessary. Opportunities to provide such structured intervention can be developed at home, in play groups/nursery or through attendance at classes provided by specialist organisations such as Tumble Tots. The activities must be progressive and broken down into small steps. Children with dyslexia can experience difficulty sequencing sounds, so it is important to limit verbal instructions. Tasks should be taught through demonstration. Early intervention can be extremely effective and the targets to be working towards for a child aged 3 are as follows:

Gross motor skills

- crawling through a tunnel (two metres length) coordinating arms and legs appropriately;

- walking backwards, forwards and sideways, arms alongside the body;

- running a distance of 10 metres without tripping or falling over;

- jumping from a low step, or on the spot with feet together;

- climbing up and down stairs in an adult fashion, placing one foot on each step;

- walking heel–toe along a measured distance of 3 metres;

- balancing along a bench/plank raised (10 cm) from the floor;

- balancing on either foot for 5 or more seconds.

Fine motor skills

- established hand preference;
- building a tower of 6 or more 2.5-cm bricks;
- reassemble a screw toy or remove the top from a jar or bottle;
- thread a determined sequence of large beads, e.g. two red, one blue, two yellow;
- complete six-piece inset puzzle/jigsaw (Figure 2.1);
- copy simple shapes, e.g. line, cross, circle, square (Figure 2.2).

Figure 2.1 **Figure 2.2**

Coordination skills

- kick a ball with either foot;
- pedal a tricycle and change direction;
- with two hands, catch a large ball thrown a distance of 3 metres (Figures 2.3, 2.4).

Figure 2.3 **Figure 2.4**

A pro-forma to assess the development of these skills is provided (Table 2.1, Figure 2.5).

Table 2.1 Skills assessment

Name_____ Age_____ Date_____

	Gross motor skills	Comments	Yes	No
1	Crawl			
2	Walk forwards backwards sideways			
3	Run			
4	Tiptoes			
5	Jump			
6	Climb			
7	Heel/toe			
8	Beam balance			
9	Balance: right foot : left foot			

Fine motor skills						
10	Handedness					
11	Tower of bricks					
12	Screw toy					
13	Bead threading					
14	Inset puzzle					
Coordination						
15	Kick: right foot / : left foot					
16	Throw: right hand / : left hand					
17	Catch (2 hands)					

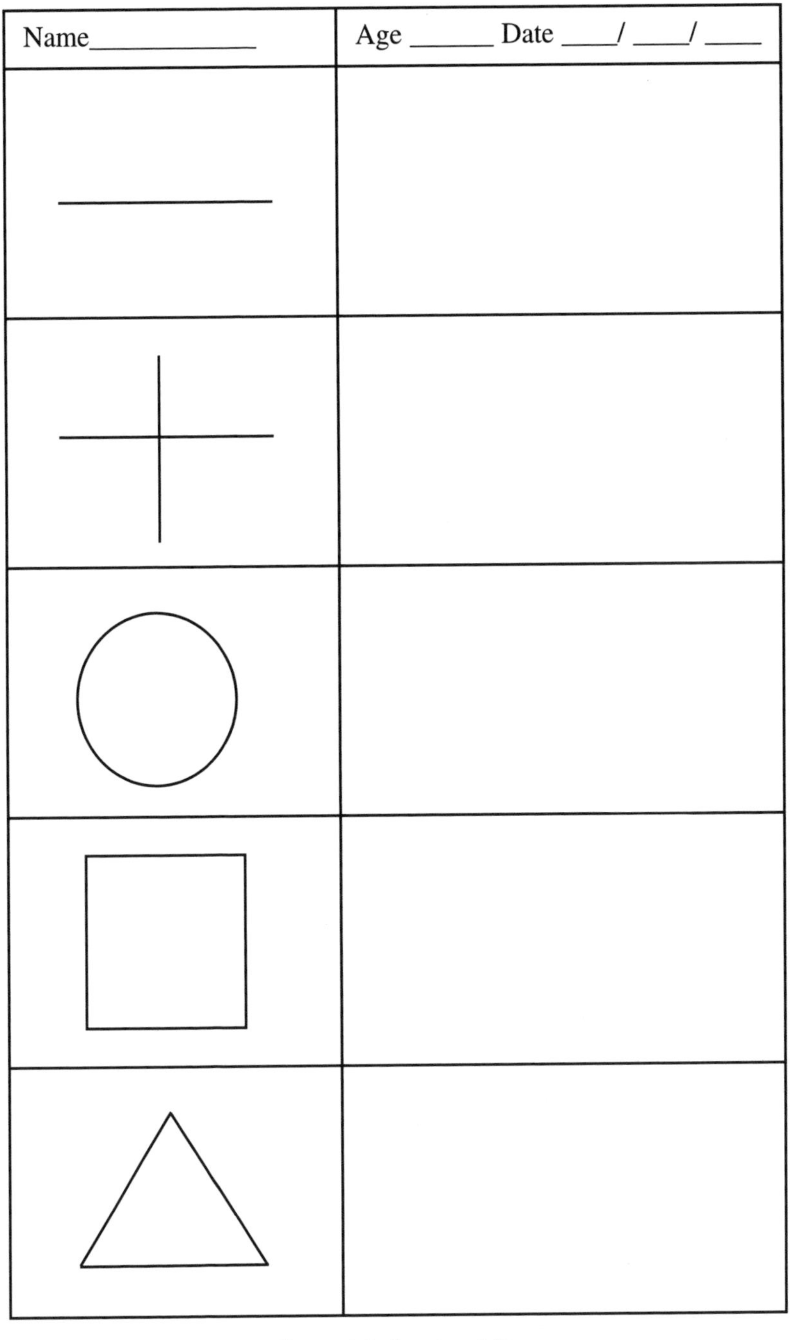

Name_____	Age _____ Date ___/ ___/ ___
———————	
+	
○	
▢	
△	

Figure 2.5 Copying skills

Structured activities to support the development of early movement skills

The activities which conclude this chapter are targeted at preschool children preparing for nursery entry at 3+ years. It is important to remember that movement skills are acquired sequentially, so any developmental programme can be accessed by children of any age at the entry point most appropriate to their ability. Although age norms are referenced in this text, its purpose is to provide programmes for skill development adapted to target the specific needs of children with dyslexia, which lead progressively to levels of competence expected in pupils of secondary age.

Children who have difficulty acquiring new skills benefit most from structured sessions because, given the freedom to choose an activity, they would avoid any that were perceived as difficult.

Very young children should be encouraged to run, jump and climb. Attractive pieces of large, colourful apparatus are evident in 'play parks', sports centres, playgroups and in many homes. Opportunities to move along beams and down slides are available almost anywhere. While they present excitement for children with competent motor skills, they can be fearful places for those who have difficulty judging heights, speed and distances or who have problems planning how to execute movement.

Perceptual skills develop alongside motor skills, and structured programmes should include both.

Control of movement begins with balance, and some children are unable to acquire the skills naturally. I have studied the Tumble Tots programme and other similar schemes that offer structured activities, which teach children the steps to achieve coordinated movement.

Bill Cosgrave, an Olympic gymnastics coach, began to develop such structured programmes in 1979, believing that physical skills are not inherited, but have to be learned. He focused particularly on tasks that would support children with perceptual motor difficulties and went on to develop the Tumble Tots activities.

The instructors are aware that there may be children in the class with specific learning difficulties and the training manual highlights the following points:

- All tasks must be demonstrated before involving the child.

- Children will respond best to tasks that are linked to their level of ability.

- Effort and success must be recognised immediately and praise should be constant.

- Tasks requiring balance, rhythm and coordination are particularly beneficial.

- To achieve automaticity, tasks involving gross and fine motor skills should be broken down into the most simple stages of progression. Opportunities to repeatedly practise the task should be given.

- Spatial and perceptual difficulties are evident in some children and there will usually be signs of poor motor organisation.

- Sequential motor tasks with a perceptual element must be broken down.

- Ball-handling skills are more than pure motor tasks and will be difficult to achieve. Careful attention to demonstrating the correct sequences of movement is essential for progress.

The activities that follow are designed for children walking independently, usually aged 18+ months to age 4.

The sessions are organised and, in part, are spent coordinating movements to music. Rhymes such as 'Head, shoulders, knees and toes' and 'The wheels on the bus' provide opportunities to develop a range of movements which, in the case of the first rhyme, are coordinated with increasing speed.

Children who have difficulties processing sounds take their cues from other children. Unfortunately, the rest of the group will be touching their toes when the first child is moving from head to shoulders.

Breaking down the sequence is important, so practise 'head' to 'shoulders' until it becomes automatic. 'Simon says' is another means of encouraging children to copy prescribed movements.

Children with specific learning difficulties benefit from multi-sensory approaches, so an adult might choose to hold the child's arms and coordinate the movements if they cannot be copied after demonstration.

The tasks also involve working with large apparatus. An ability to move all four limbs separately is fundamental to the development of competent motor skills. As mentioned earlier, possibly 80 per cent of children with specific learning difficulties do not crawl as babies. The easiest way to assess and develop these skills is to encourage the child to move through a circular or box tunnel (Figure 2.6).

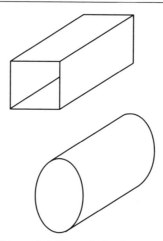

Figure 2.6 Box and circular tunnel

The box tunnel is designed for the early toddler and incorporates two different heights. Simple activities such as walking along a measured line heel/toe become more complex when the child is asked to carry a bean bag under his/her chin: balance skills are extended further by repeating the activity on a balance beam (Figure 2.7).

Figure 2.7 Balance beam.

The beam rests on the floor between two supports and comprises interchangeable walking surfaces. To facilitate the progressive acquisition of skills a 10 cm width reduces to 5 cm as the child becomes more competent.

When engaging in balance activities, the children are initially encouraged to keep their arms close to the body. As skills develop, they are able to extend their arms outwards, upwards and in opposition to one another.

The Meccano® Walk (Figure 2.8) is an extension of the balance beam. The walking surface is raised from the ground and the child is required to change direction while balancing.

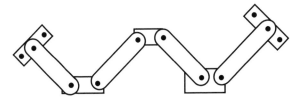

Figure 2.8 The Meccano® Walk

Eye–foot coordination is developed using stepping-stones (Figure 2.9). The body position moves from the right to left side as the child moves along the steps. Children with dyslexia experience problems when an additional task is added, for example collecting a beanbag from a basket at one end and carrying it to a basket at the other. These activities need to be mastered and, with sufficient opportunity to practise, the skill will be learned.

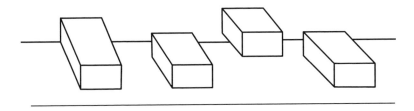

Figure 2.9 Stepping-stones

Team games – passing a ball along the line over heads and between legs, and collaborative working – using a parachute present problems. The children are not only executing simple movements over which they have sole control, they have to interpret and act on the movement of other children. Breaking down the sequences will be discussed in Chapter 3.

Perceptual skills are also an area of focus during the session. One example is the target board (Figure 2.10).
The target board stands at two-thirds body height of the children, and activities range from 'posting' beanbags into named spaces – square, triangle etc. – to fitting handled inset pieces which match the shapes.

Encourage the child to experience different textures, touching them with hands and feet. Develop simple balance activities, standing on a hard surface, a sponge mat and in sand.

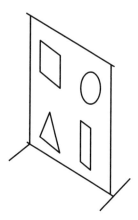

Figure 2.10 Target board

The examples given in this chapter are selected from a range of possible activities. It is important to set achievable targets to encourage the child to further develop their skills.

Chapter 3

Activities for Children in the Nursery

The assessment of motor skills described in the previous chapter measures the competencies that should be evident given the children's expected neurological and physiological development. However, any screening of this population currently attending nursery or playgroups would yield a significant proportion unable to complete many of these tasks. In the majority of cases, it is due to lack of experience; the children have not had sufficient opportunity to practise their movement skills. Entry to nursery can provide opportunities to develop abilities but this must be carried out in a structured way. It is important to cover the aspects of development that may have been 'missed' in the early years. It can no longer be left to chance (Wetton 1997) because the ability to coordinate movement and develop perceptual skills is fundamental to further learning experiences. The child needs to begin to express his/her ideas, firstly through drawing and then writing. Children who have perceptual and coordination difficulties in their early development struggle to produce legible handwriting. The problems are exacerbated as the children progress from Foundation Stage through the other key stages as the requirement for written work increases.

The development of good perceptual and motor skills has a direct effect on the development of handwriting (Portwood 1999). The nursery environment provides an excellent opportunity to take preventative steps before the children have had a chance to fail.

Many children who in later years display classical signs of dyslexia show evidence of problems by age 3. Low-level intervention at this stage can have a significant effect on future learning.

In all of the suggested activities, it is important to be aware that many children with dyslexia will have:

- reduced visual motor sensitivity;

- unsteady visual perception;

- problems with convergence; and

- reduced sensitivity to changes in sound frequency.

(Stein 2002)

This in turn will affect their ability to:

- judge speed

    - how fast they are travelling in relation to objects and people in the space around them;

    - how quickly a ball, for example, is travelling towards them;

- judge distances

    - how far away the ground might be when they jump from the top of a climbing frame;

    - how to plan movements to jump in and out of hoops;

    - how to throw and kick accurately at targets;

    - how to move safely between objects without bumping into them or falling;

- focus on the task

    - convergence difficulties may result in 'double vision' making it more difficult to plan where the body or object might be;

- respond to verbal instructions quickly

    - the class is given the instruction to change direction: everyone else turns, the dyslexic child does not;

    - sequencing sounds/rhythms to movements such as taking an active part in marching or performing actions in response to a beat.

Any programme should include activities that will focus and develop these particular skills. It is very important that the children do not feel singled out and different from the rest of the group. The whole class should be able to join in – but there are a few points to remember:

- Keep the use of language to a minimum;

- Always demonstrate the task, either yourself, or ask a child who has been observed as competent in the skill;

- Use visual cues – don't say 'Find a space'; place coloured spots or markers down;

- Break down the task into small, achievable targets;

- Make sure that each skill is learned separately before using them in combinations – the child must be able to balance (both feet flat on the floor and then on each leg (5+ seconds)) before hopping and skipping, as these skills are acquired separately.

The progression in development of movement skills will be discussed in more detail in the next chapter.

The following suggestions are activities that can be set up in the nursery to target the possible areas of difficulty previously highlighted. They are divided into three groups, to extend:

- motor skills;

- perceptual skills; and

- coordination.

The children will normally work individually, although there are some occasions when pairing (one child modelling good skills) can support the development of a child who is having difficulties.

Motor skills

Encourage the children to move in different ways. Begin with a steady walk forwards – mark the direction of travel and use coloured cones or spots. Introduce listening skills and instruct the children to walk forwards after five beats, tapped on a tambourine, for example. A further tap indicates 'stop'. Use terms such as 'high', 'low', 'tall', 'short'. Ask the children to walk tall on their toes and then crouch down. Demonstrate the movements and then ask the children to copy.

When the children have mastered these movements, direct them to change their speed. A slow walk, more quickly, then jogging. Extend skills by describing different types of movement:

- rolling

- slithering

- jumping (feet together – bunny jump)

- crawling (hands and knees, then hands and feet).

When the movement is mastered, include directional changes. Forwards, backwards, side-steps between parallel lines. Tape zig-zags onto the floor. Use coloured discs or beanbags. 'Move to a yellow circle'. Use visual cues. Rubber foot templates give excellent visual representation of 'small', 'medium' and 'giant' strides (Figure 3.1). Trails can be made from skipping ropes.

Set up a simple circuit – (Figure 3.2). Choose perhaps a series of 'walking' activities, e.g. setting off from the red disc, moving forwards,

Figure 3.1

walk heel–toe along a measured line of 3 metres. From the green disc, move feet, taking sideways steps between parallel lines 20 cm apart for a distance of 3 metres. From the yellow disc, still walking forwards, follow the zig-zag onto the measured lines, 3 metres, walking forwards with each foot on the opposite side of the line, i.e. the right edge of the right foot touching the left edge of the line and vice versa (Figure 3.3). 'Stepping stones' follow: and back to the start.

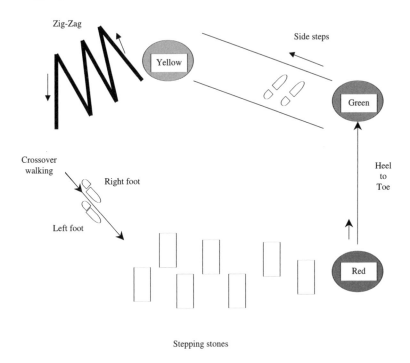

Figure 3.2 Circuit layout

The same circuit can be developed to involve:

- tip toes
- running
- forwards on some tasks, backwards on others
- stretching high
- creeping
- turning
- moving in time to rhythm.

Extension activities could include changing heights. Use benches and alter the angle of the slope. Again, encourage the children to walk forwards, backwards and sideways.

Figure 3.3

In developing basic motor skills, it is important to introduce an element that increases stamina. Activities such as jumping and running improve muscle strength and tone, and develop breathing skills. This becomes more important with age and will be discussed in more detail in later chapters.

Perceptual skills
Ability to judge speed, distance and height depends on perceptual awareness. Understanding of shapes allows a child to judge his/her position in space – can they pass without bumping into another person or object?

These skills are developed with practice; much of it trial and error. The young child will scramble to the top of the climbing frame and launch him/herself from the top, not realising that the ground is relatively far away. They pedal a tricycle at speed, unaware that the faster they go, the sooner they reach a fence or wall.

In early development, the child starts to make reaching and grasping movements towards objects of interest, – a mobile, a familiar face. Every so often, just by chance initially, contact is made between the child and object. As success is repeated, the 'planning' of the movement becomes automatic. So fixation on the object and the positioning of the shoulder, arm and wrist, to make contact, becomes programmed – not only for a range of distances but also to take into account the speed of movement between the body and the object: like catching a ball or scoring a goal.

In these early years, easily achievable targets are important: a young child can be encouraged to 'blow bubbles' and then 'pop' them, clapping hands together. The bubbles move slowly and allow for the 'planning time' necessary to track their movement. The child becomes more competent with practice and learns to position his/her body high, low and from one side to the other. They learn to 'fixate' and respond instinctively (Figures 3.4 and 3. 5).

Many dyslexic children and adults have particular difficulty assessing object distance (problems with convergence) and the time it will take if travelling to move from point 'A' to point 'B' (reduced visual motion sensitivity). Activities that support the development of perceptual skills should be included within the programme of physical education.

Figure 3.4   **Figure 3.5**

The focus of these activities is to explore shape and space: young children need a point of reference to keep them in the 'right' place. The space should be confined to a rubber disc or a hoop, next to a marker (Figure 3.6).

27

Figure 3.6

The children will be developing their basic motor skills such as running, hopping, as discussed earlier, so they can be incorporated into a perceptual activity. They can hop or jump from one spot (lily pad) to another, without landing in the 'water'. Increase the distance between the spots. The children have to plan their moves to accommodate the change. Jumping 'cleanly' from one spot (hoop) to another may take time, but it is important to keep practising until this skill can generalise to different movements – hopping, jumping between varying distances (Figure 3.7).

Figure 3.7

Extension activities could involve moving between spots with low-level obstacles separating them, e.g. cones, benches.

Children with perceptual-motor problems find it difficult to move safely at speed from one point to another. Build these skills slowly. Identify points around the area. Ask the children to move slowly between these points, on command, without touching one another. Not only are they making judgements about their own position, but also they have to consider the movements of other children and avoid them. As the children become more competent, they can increase the speed of their movements.

The following activities are designed to focus specifically on improving the child's ability to judge distances.

Start by using a large container: the child throws a beanbag into it, right hand then left, with increasing distance from the target. In the early stages beanbags are preferable to balls – less time is spent chasing them! Skittles are fun and provide a measure of improvement. How many can be knocked over each time? Varying the size of the ball and the distance to be rolled increases the level of difficulty. After rolling, the activity can extend to kicking a ball at a target or between two measured points. Encourage the child to use both feet.

The floor gives the child another reference point so, to develop skills further, the targets can be raised. The ball can be thrown into a hoop or aimed at an object placed on a shelf. Beanbags thrown at stacked containers is a very popular game.

The children should begin to work collaboratively with each other and they can begin by simply rolling a large sponge ball to one another while in a V-shaped sitting position. Then progress to standing balance; the children throw and catch a ball to one another using a two-handed pass. It is important to match the skills of both children to alleviate the frustration of the task continually breaking down.

Another activity, which can be enjoyed by the whole class, is to play 'Simon says'. The children are copying movements demonstrated by the adult. Visual feedback helps children with planning difficulties and the game encourages them to develop their listening skills. Begin the game very slowly at first and use simple movements such as 'hands on your head', 'touch your toes', 'lift one leg'. When response times are within seconds, instructions can be given more quickly: this in turn improves automatisation.

Coordination

The term 'motor skills' generally applies to activities such as rolling, running and throwing. When these fundamental skills are combined together – for example a hop, skip and a jump – the result is a coordinated action. An element of coordination is involved when there is more than one dimension to the task. Throwing a ball is a motor skill; throwing a ball into a hoop requires coordination.

Riding a bike is a coordinated activity: pedalling with a foot, steering with arms and hands while judging the speed and distance travelled. The nursery can provide opportunities to use sit-astride toys, and those accommodating more than one child allow just for the movement of the legs, initially, without having to worry about steering. With developing competence, the children can take turns to be the driver (Figure 3.8).

Fawcett and Nicolson (1996), and Fawcett *et al.* (2001) refer to the 'double deficit' of dyslexia, and children who, in addition to having problems with literacy, had problems with balance, 'especially if they were prevented from concentrating on their balance by having to perform another task at the same time' (Fawcett 2001). Coordination presents particular problems for these dyslexic children. With practice, 'performance can become automatic', but, strikingly, a 'square root rule' suggests that this takes longer in proportion to the square root of the time normally taken to acquire a skill. So a simple skill that normally takes four sessions to master, would take a dyslexic child eight sessions, whereas if it normally took 400 sessions it would take the dyslexic child 8,000 sessions (Fawcett 2001).

Quite clearly, this has huge implications for the development of physical skills. If the time taken to acquire skills is so much greater, the element of 'trial and error' must be overcome. This is best

Figure 3.8

achieved by providing a school-based motor programme that focuses on the development of balance, coordination and perceptual skills (possible areas of difficulty) while still allowing the child to progress with ' motor skills', those least likely to be affected.

Returning to the discussion that began in the introduction to this book, do children with dyslexia necessarily have problems with Physical Education? Can this be the case when there are notable sportsmen and sportswomen who are themselves dyslexic?

Closer examination of their skills, perhaps, provides some answers. There are few 'team players': the majority are involved in sports requiring high levels of strength and stamina, good balance and basic motor-skill development. They are swimmers, divers, rowers, a decathlon gold medallist and a world martial arts champion.

Spatial ability and coordination are less important, so if children with dyslexia are encouraged to practise their balance and develop basic motor skills, perhaps they are more likely to develop greater levels of competence.

The answer, it seems, is for educators to encourage the development of these skills and to provide structured opportunities to improve perception and coordination through activities, which are broken down into developmental stages.

From the work of Fawcett and Nicolson, however, children require repeated opportunities to practise newly acquired skills so that they can become automatic.

At the end of nursery, children should have established 'handedness'. They should prefer using one or the other. It can be difficult to judge, but a simple assessment can provide this information. Take a sheet of carbonised paper and draw a circle 8 cm in diameter. Seat the child at a table with the circle placed centrally in front of him/her (Figure 3.9). Give the child a striking object (the

Figure 3.9

small hammers supplied with trays of toffee are ideal), firstly in his/her right hand. Ask the child to try and hit the centre of the circle as many times as possible in 20 attempts. Replace the paper and repeat the activity using the left hand. Examination of the marks reveals the hand which was most competent (Figure 3.10). In this case it was the left hand.

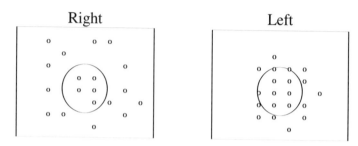

Figure 3.10

This assessment can also be used with older pupils. It is important that when a child moves into Reception Class that drawing and writing implements are placed in the preferred hand.

Chapter 4

An Introduction to Movement Skills from Foundation to Key Stage 2

Chapters 5, 6 and 7 provide structured programmes of activities to develop the balance, basic motor and coordination skills in children from Foundation through KS2. This chapter focuses on the principles of the movement programme.

It is the first day in school after the summer break. The Reception class teacher introduces each of the children to the rest of the group. There is great variation between the pupils: some have just turned four, others are rapidly approaching their fifth birthday. It is difficult not to be aware of the differences in maturation, particularly between the boys and girls. These developmental differences persist often into late teenage years and maturation is one of the most important factors when assessing the physical skills of a child, particularly when there is evidence of specific learning difficulties. The development of skills is progressive and they are acquired sequentially. A child will find it impossible to hop if he/she is unable to balance. Independent movement of arms and legs must be achieved before swimming strokes can be mastered.

Differing levels of maturity and the time to develop new physical skills varies greatly between individuals. Many children with dyslexia need to practise a new skill for much longer than their peers (Fawcett's (2001) 'square root rule') before they become competent.

In addition, the skills must be broken down into their components and taught sequentially. It is therefore unrealistic to make statements that specify expected skill acquisition at particular key stages, as skills will be acquired at different rates.

The purpose of this section is to break down motor skills into their developmental stages and to suggest teaching approaches that support learning. In this way 'progression' can be measured, and there will be a means of determining rate of learning. As discussed in the previous chapter, not all children with dyslexia find the development of motor skills problematic: by providing a developmental scheme of working, the child is given personal targets against which to measure progress. In areas in which they show greater levels of competence they will achieve the targets and acquire 'new skills' more quickly. Also, by separating out the areas on which to work into balance, motor skills and coordination, it is possible to excel in one, e.g. running (motor skill), while extending abilities in others. It is very important that children are allowed to excel in physical activities when they show levels of competence. So often, children with learning difficulties are removed from classes where they are doing well to spend time completing remedial work to support other aspects of learning. It must be possible to do both!

How to use the programme

Each section starts with basic skills, some of which should have been acquired before entering school. This ensures a 'complete' programme of development. It is very difficult to learn new skills when there are 'gaps' in earlier stages. Each target should be achieved before moving on to the next. The activities are designed so that they can be incorporated into a 'whole-class' PE session, although you may decide to provide the child experiencing difficulties with additional 'practice' time and set up a lunchtime or out-of-school club.

It is important that any club is not given a label, that would associate it with 'failure', like 'Club for the uncoordinated' (it has been known!). One school invited children to attend the '10.40 Club' at break time; another was just called 'Fit for fun'.

The activities are progressive and the skills identified reflect targets proposed by the DfES for PE from Foundation through to Key Stage 3. The secondary curriculum is discussed separately in

Chapter 8. However, given that by the end of KS2, in a class of 10/11-year-olds, there will probably be different maturational levels between children, the DfES targets should provide a reference point rather than expectation of achievement.

Regardless of the child's chronological age, he/she should access a physical education programme that takes into account his/her maturation (physiological/neurological competence) and ability. Children with specific learning difficulties will be at varying stages of development, depending on the activity, e.g. motor skills may be well in advance of coordination.

The aim of physical education is to develop the purposeful control of body movement. First, personal control must be mastered, but this can be developed into collaborative relationships, where it is necessary to be able to predict the movements of others: a game of tennis, football or, perhaps, a contact sport.

The DfES Guidance divides PE into the following sections:

- Dance
- Games
- Gymnastics
- Athletics
- Swimming
- Invasion games
- Striking and fielding games
- Net/wall games
- Outdoor and adventurous activities

They can all be categorised under three basic headings.

Balance – the ability to remain in place while stretching/bending the body into different shapes. For example, standing feet together, on one leg/heel, or perhaps completing a handstand.

Motor skills – basic repetitive movements. For example, running, jumping, throwing.

Coordination – when two or more different movements are combined and they can cover a range of activities, many with a perceptual component. For example, walking heel–toe along a measured line, combining three basic movements into a hop, skip and a jump, or throwing a ball at a target – the requirement to aim the ball into a specified space introduces another 'planning' element into the motor skill.

Where children with dyslexia appear to experience the greatest difficulty is when the movement is other than repetitive. Where the same action, e.g. running, rowing, is processed over and over again, automatisation is achieved quickly: this enables the child to become competent and excel.

Balance skills, although a more difficult task for some children, can be mastered when the skills are presented in small, progressive steps: with repeated opportunities to practise, high levels of skill can be achieved.

Coordinated activities are most problematic: from the discussion in previous chapters, the child struggling to develop movement skills needs to repeat the same task over and over again until it becomes 'stored' and then processed instinctively. If the ability to 'plan' movements does not generalise to new situations – e.g. a ball is thrown to the left instead of the right, and the child must move in the opposite way to catch – there are huge implications for the amount of time required to learn a 'new skill' where an element of coordination is required.

It seems, therefore, that the focus for the development of movement skills by the end of KS2 should be to enable the child to achieve a general level of all-round competence, with opportunities to practise balance and motor activities, which could then be 'chosen' from a range of options more readily available in secondary education.

What to look for

As you observe the child developing their movement skills, you will see some evidence of associated movements: when running, their arms may wave around; when jumping their elbows may be in the air; their arms could lift out at either side when doing sideways steps. These additional, involuntary movements can get in the way when the child is learning a new skill. It can help if, for example, the child is given something to hold – a large ball, perhaps, will keep hands and arms in close to the chest and so jumping feet together becomes more coordinated. The appropriate movements are then reinforced. In the sections which follow there are many examples of movement difficulties and strategies which have proved helpful to many children.

It is recommended that children change for PE. Young children, and those with coordination difficulties, often spend more time with this task than participating in the lesson. Just finding a way round this problem can dramatically reduce stress levels for many of them: you may decide that just a change of footwear is appropriate for some sessions, or that children who struggle to dress in the time allocated are allowed a break or time during lunch to do so.

Warming up and cooling down

All sessions should begin and end with a series of stretching activities regardless of the ages of the children. The suggestions, which follow, start at a basic level and are progressive.

The first set of photographs show Reception/Year 1 children and then Year 4/5 pupils engaging in more advanced stretching. Children of any age, or even adults, should be involved in activities appropriate for their level of development: this is the case for all of the recommendations made in this book. Photographs have been used to illustrate some of the points raised.

Sequencing instructions, relayed verbally and converted into planned movements, can present some difficulties. Always demonstrate the moves, either by yourself or using a child who is competent in that skill. Videos are useful and they can be replayed for children who require additional processing time. This provides visual reinforcement, which will help all of the children, not just those with specific learning difficulties.

Activities

1. 'Find a space'
   - use visual cues, coloured discs, markers on the floor, and direct children to places in the room;

2. Sit on the floor
   - stretch out legs and toes, move toes independently, feel muscles tense and then relax;

3. Stand, feet together

    – stretch arms, in front, behind, outstretch to the sides

    – relax arms, move fingers independently, curl fingers moving
       eventually into a fisted shape;

4. Standing, placing hands on the waist and rotate hips – one
    direction then the other (Figure 4.1);

Figure 4.1 Hip rotation

5. Standing still – stretch arms to shoulder height and rotate from
    the waist; change directions;

6. Standing, feet together, bend and, placing hands on knees, rotate
    one way then the other (Figure 4.2);

Figure 4.2

7.   After demonstration (Figure 4.3), encourage the children to bend sideways, left and right, reaching as far as they can go (Figure 4.4);

Figure 4.3

Figure 4.4

8.   Extend the activity, lifting the opposite arm over the head, reaching as near as possible to their feet (Figures 4.5 and 4.6);

Figure 4.5

Figure 4.6

9.   Move on to the leg stretches (Figures 4.7 and 4.8): right leg bent at the knee with the left leg stretched back and the converse with right leg back;

Figure 4.7   Figure 4.8

10. Bending from the waist (Figures 4.9 and 4.10), stretch down towards the right foot then towards the left.

Figure 4.9   Figure 4.10

11. Forward stretches: young children find it difficult to sit on the floor, legs outstretched with the back of their knees touching the ground. Begin by asking the children to sit forwards, legs in a 'V' shape and encourage them to maintain their balance in this position. Holding a large sponge ball close to the chest enables children who are experiencing difficulties to achieve better sitting balance (Figure 4.11).

Figure 4.11

12. As skills develop, encourage the children to sit on the floor, legs straight and arms extending to touch toes (Figure 4.12). Visual feedback supports pupils with specific learning difficulties and attempts to reach an upturned cup or box placed on a book/board over the feet provide a great visual incentive to stretch further (Figure 4.13).

Figure 4.12   **Figure 4.13**

Chapter 5

Developing Skills – Balance

When demonstrating movements, make sure you have the child's attention: mention names; identify a child who is trying hard:

1. Demonstrate the expected starting position: make sure it is secure because it is the starting point for most movement sequences.

    Feet together, toes pointing forwards, arms alongside the body with head and eyes facing forwards. Place a target on the wall to focus on or wear a shirt bearing a logo at the children's eye level (Figure 5.1).

    Ask the children to move their hands with fingers slightly curved towards their chins with elbows tucked in (Figure 5.2).

    Support: if the child has difficulty achieving this position and maintaining balance, give him/her a sponge ball to hold at chin height. This allows arms to be in the correct position and stops them from producing associated movements (Figure 5.3).

2. Feet together, hands positioned centrally, the children lift onto their toes and then back to the soles of their feet.

    Support: if the child wobbles, he/she can hold a sponge ball centrally to his/her chest. This improves balance.

3. Feet together, the children move onto their toes, stretching their arms above their heads (Figure 5.4).

Figure 5.1

Figure 5.2

Figure 5.3

Figure 5.4

Support: A marker or disc helps the child to keep on the same spot.

4. When standing balance is achieved, move on to one-leg balance. Begin with hands positioned centrally and demonstrate raising one foot from the floor.

   Figure 5.5 depicts a child trying to achieve one-foot static balance: he is unsteady and is unable to maintain this position for more than 3+ seconds. Figure 5.6 shows the child holding

 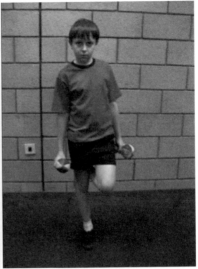

Figure 5.5   **Figure 5.6**

beanbags, one in either hand. Good static balance of 10+ seconds is now achieved.

During whole-class PE sessions, it is easy to identify the children who have problems with balance (Figure 5.7). The child on the left in this picture is showing associated arm movements. She, too, will achieve more competent balance skills if she is given beanbags or a large ball to hold.

As skills develop, the leg can be raised higher.

Support: A beanbag placed on the foot helps the child control the leg/foot position (Figure 5.8). As the child becomes more competent, he/she can be encouraged to bend forward from the waist and touch the toes of the extended leg (Figure 5.9).

Support: Steady the child by holding the elbow of the opposing arm. Work gradually towards achieving higher levels of competence (Figure 5.10).

5. From standing position, balance on one leg and bend the knee of the other. Practise lifting the foot up behind the body initially (Figure 5.11) then move on to 'high knee' lifting. With the knee still bent, bring the leg out in front of the body and lift towards waist height.

Support: Where children experience difficulty maintaining balance, allow them to rest the raised foot on a small object

Figure 5.7

Figure 5.8

Figure 5.9

Figure 5.10

initially (tennis ball), and then to a large ball as the child becomes more competent (Figure 5.12).

Extension activities would involve a high knee position and lifting from the sole to the ball of the foot remaining on the floor.

(a) Older and more competent pupils can then develop a range of arm positions, both extended outwards

(Figure 5.12), one high, one low (Figure 5.13), incorporating twisting from the waist.

Pupils should now be able to identify their own points for visual fixation.

Support: Problems with convergence may continue to affect balance: encourage a child with these difficulties to identify a large, easily visible, focus.

6. When the pupils can balance on a solid floor, change textures using foam mats and then use a range of heights and shapes.

Figure 5.11

Figure 5.12   **Figure 5.13**

Blocks lined up on the floor are suitable for KS1 children. The child in Figure 5.14 is concentrating on balancing heel–toe and his fists are clenched and held downwards from the waist – his balance is quite unsteady.

Support: Beanbags or quoits (Figure 5.15) held in outstretched hands give greater stability.

Figure 5.14

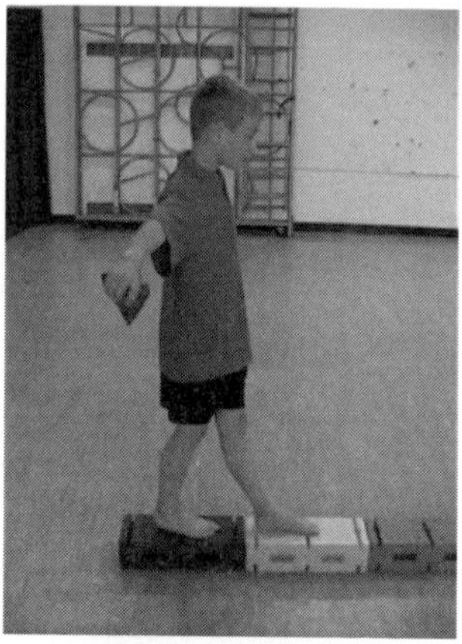

Figure 5.15

Figure 5.16 shows Year 3 pupils balancing, feet together, on a wooden bench. The pupil on the left of the picture would also benefit from holding objects in both hands.

Year 5 pupils are using the surface of a sloping bench to balance (Figure 5.17). The angle of slope can be gradually increased. Standing sideways and backwards is also an extension activity.

Figure 5.16

Figure 5.17

7.   Large soft balls are very popular with children and provide further opportunities to develop balance skills. In the pictures (Figures 5.18 and 5.19), a Year 3 pupil balances, feet on the floor and arms holding the side of the ball. He extends his arms and requires a little support to balance. Figure 5.20 depicts a Year 5 pupil who is competent with single-leg balance.

Wobble boards are great fun for younger children. Begin with a short plank over a cylinder. The child learns to move weight

Figure 5.18

Figure 5.19

Figure 5.20

from one foot to the other. Circular boards on which a small ball can be rolled around the circumference of the board develop a child's ability to find his/her position in space and make appropriate body adjustments to remain upright.

8. At the end of KS2, pupils should be developing balance skills that extend arms and legs in opposing directions. Figure 5.21 shows Year 5 children attempting one-leg forward balance with arms outstretched.

    The pupils work collaboratively, and in doing so improve and develop skills (Figure 5.22). With targets broken down into small, achievable steps, and repeated opportunities to practise, even youngsters with initial motor learning difficulties can achieve high levels of competence (Figures 5.23 and 5.24).

Figure 5.21

Figure 5.22

Figure 5.23

Figure 5.24

Balance skills at the end of primary and the start of secondary education extend to tasks that introduce weight bearing through arms as well as legs.

Chapter 6

Developing Skills – Movement

This chapter focuses on the acquisition of basic movement skills. 'Stretching', described in the previous chapter, should be carried out before involving the children in more rigorous activities.

1. Instruct the children to 'find a space' and 'walk round the room'. Make the direction of travel clear and make sure that arm movements are coordinated.

   Support: children who have difficulty moving arms and legs together benefit from holding quoits.

2. Change the direction of movement: forwards, backwards, sideways.

   Support: You will observe that some children raise their arms to waist height when walking sideways (Figure 6.1). Beanbags and quoits are probably not quite heavy enough to overcome the associated movements and bring arms down to the side of the body. Give the child batons or small-handled, liquid/sand-filled plastic juice cartons to hold, one in each hand (Figure 6.2).

It is important that inappropriate movements in these basic skills are corrected.

3. Introduce an element of speed. Select movements from (2) and encourage the child to move more quickly.

Support: With young children and those who have difficulty maintaining their position in space, it is useful to mark areas on the floor with instructions for the direction of travel. Use straight or parallel lines, instructing the child to keep alongside or within them. A skipping-rope provides a 'curved' path.

Figure 6.1   Figure 6.2

4. Now ask the children to display a range of heights and widths: 'Make yourself as tall as you can, as short or as wide' (Figure 6.3).

Figure 6.3

Support: Demonstrate 'crouching' and extend arms demonstrating 'wide'. When movement is introduced remember that many children with dyslexia have difficulty with motion sensitivity: they are unable to judge speed and distance and may not be deliberately 'crashing' into the child next to them. Mark their boundaries: 'Only move between the red and yellow spots'.

5. Ask the children to walk on their toes and introduce listening skills. They can slide or walk on the balls of their feet. Say 'Make sure I can't hear your steps'. Change direction, introduce swirling and spinning.

    Support: Many children with dyslexia have problems associated with balance and the middle ear. A couple of twirls can totally disorientate them. Insist that the children twirl only a short distance (2 m) and mark it with cones or lines. Ensure that 'stationary' activities come between those with turning movements.

6. Let the children explore movement along the surface of the floor. For some activities you will need to use foam mats: encourage the children to crawl, roll (Figure 6.4) or pull themselves along by their hands.

Figure 6.4

Support: It is very important to examine the children's crawling movements. More than 80 per cent of children subsequently identified with a neurodevelopmental disorder (dyslexia, dyspraxia, ADHD, Autistic Spectrum Disorder) do not go through

55

the crawling stage as babies. Observation of their movements will show a range of immaturities, which should be corrected. Figure 6.5 shows a child moving with his feet held upwards and off the floor. The second picture (Figure 6.6) shows the hands turned inwards, fingers pointing towards the body.

Figure 6.5   **Figure 6.6**

It is important to ensure that the correct crawling position is learned: feet resting on the floor with the palm of the hands flat, fingers pointing away from the body.

7. As an extension of walking, ask the children to march either in a circle or between designated 'spots'. Make sure that arms move in opposition, i.e. right arm with left leg. Develop listening skills and instruct the children to start and stop on command: change direction and alter speed.

    Support: Some children may find it difficult to move arms and legs in opposition. A baton or quoit held in the hand emphasises the swing of the arms. This can help the child to develop the correct movement pattern.

8. 'Jumping' has four different take-off and landing possibilities:

    (a)   2-foot take-off, 2-foot land

    (b)   2-foot take-off, 1-foot land

    (c)   1-foot take-off, 2-foot land

    (d)   1-foot take-off, 1-foot land.

    A hop comprises a jump that has single-foot take-off and the same-foot land. Hopping is a sequence of one-foot jumps.

Skipping is a sequence of single-foot take-off and single-foot landing, using alternative feet.

Support: If the child jumps 2-foot take-off, 2-foot land (Figure 6.7) with his arms flailing, give him beanbags to hold in each hand (Figure 6.8).

Figure 6.7   **Figure 6.8**

Hopping (1-foot take-off, 1-foot land) will probably produce similar hand movements (Figure 6.9). Again, give the child something to hold – a large sponge ball close to the chest (Figure 6.10) or quoits/beanbags to keep his hands down.

Younger children can be encouraged to sequence their hops by putting them into a 'rain dance'.

9. An extension activity is to use a small trampoline to practise jumping.

    Support: Use beanbags to reduce associated movement in the arms (Figures 6.11 and 6.12).

10. Incorporate 'twisting' from side to side while jumping on the trampoline.

    Support: It may be necessary to provide low-level support by holding the wrist. This enables the child to maintain his/her 'position in space' (Figure 6.13).

Figure 6.9

Figure 6.10

Figure 6.11

Figure 6.12

11. The next stage is to incorporate an obstacle into the jump. Reception and Year 1 children can jump over a line or into a hoop from a low step. Years 2/3/4 can jump over a skipping rope (Figure 6.14) – a one-leg take-off and 2-foot landing.

Years 5/6 can jump over small hurdles and sequence several jumps together. This is good preparation for the 'high jump' in secondary school.

Figure 6.13

Figure 6.14

Support: The children will progress if the movement is learned properly at the beginning. Increase the height gradually: the child can be set personal targets.

12. Rolling – demonstrate a 'log roll' (Figure 6.4) and encourage the children to copy with arms outstretched or alongside the body. Demonstrate a 'drop-shoulder' roll (Figures 6.15 and 6.16). In the photo, the left elbow is tucked into the waist and the left

shoulder touches the mat. The child rolls over onto his/her back, making sure that the head does not make contact with the floor. Following the demonstration, the children copy (Figure 6.17).

Figure 6.15   Figure 6.16   Figure 6.17

The forward roll should be demonstrated (Figures 6.18 and 6.19). The head is tucked between the knees but raised from the floor. The legs straighten from the knees and weight is taken onto the hands.

The body is propelled onto the back again without the head touching the mat. Children must be observed carefully when completing a forward roll (Figures 6.20 and 6.21).

Figure 6.18   Figure 6.19

Figure 6.20

Figure 6.21

Support: When children do not listen and follow the demonstration, they are more likely to place the tops of their heads on the mat and attempt to balance on it while flinging their legs into the air in an attempt to push over onto their backs. Many less-well-coordinated children have been observed attempting a forward roll in this fashion.

Pre-school children benefit from 'rolling' over large cylinders of soft play equipment. Start early, encouraging them to tuck their heads in and land on their backs, instead of balancing on their heads.

The last example is the 'teddy-bear roll'. The children adopt a V-shaped sitting position with hands holding the underside of the calf as close to the ankle as possible (Figure 6.22). Maintaining the triangular leg shape, roll onto the back and pivot towards the right (Figure 6.23).

Figure 6.22

Figure 6.23

Make sure everyone is moving the same way. Roll forwards, legs kept in position, and sit upright again on the mat (Figure 6.24).

Figure 6.24

The photographs show Year 5/6 pupils not quite mastering the task, but it is good preparation for the secondary PE curriculum.

> *Support*: Using apparatus improves balance, strength and coordination, the activities can involve climbing, balancing, (Figure 6.25), walking, running and crawling.

The development of motor skills forms the basis of the athletics and gymnastics curriculum in secondary school.

Figure 6.25

Chapter 7

Developing Skills – Coordination

A coordinated activity is one that involves two or more processes. For example: throwing a ball is a motor skill; throwing a ball at a target is a coordination skill. It is coordinated activities that present the greatest difficulties to children with dyslexia: it is important, therefore, to master the motor skills first.

A nine-year-old dyslexic pupil in a mainstream primary school had developed a high level of competency jumping sequentially, two-foot take-off, two-foot landing, between six hoops placed in a straight row (Figure 7.1).

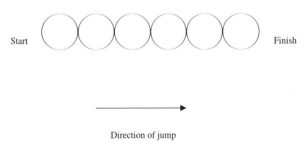

Start   Finish

Direction of jump

Figure 7.1

The hoops were then placed in a zig-zag formation (Figure 7.2) and 'Tom', after several attempts and some initial hesitancy, jumped competently from start to finish, changing direction with each jump.

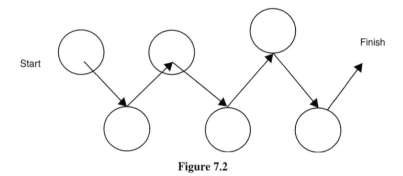

Figure 7.2

The natural extension of this exercise was to arrange a number of hoops of two different colours, and Tom was asked to jump from start to finish without standing in any of those coloured yellow (Figure 7.3).

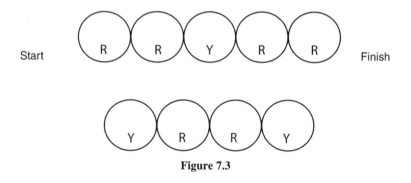

Figure 7.3

Tom froze; he looked up and down the line, trying to plan his moves in advance. He stood in the first red hoop and looked at each of the three adjoining hoops in turn. He was unable to jump; it was just about all he could manage to step from one to another. With each step he showed obvious associated movements in his hands. A right-legged step produced a raised right arm and hand; a left-legged step the opposite.

Tom was given wooden batons, one to hold in each hand. He started the task again and stepped freely from one red hoop to the next. After some repetition of this task, he was able to jump slowly between the required hoops. He practised this activity with several others every day for a week. At the end of this time he could perform the moves competently, without batons and without any evidence of associated movements.

Fawcett and Nicolson (1996) identified similar problems in a group of dyslexic children they were studying.

Balance and motor skills must be secure before attempting more complex coordination tasks, which must be broken down into small achievable targets.

Gymnastics links together movement sequences. Children can incorporate a 'run and a jump', then, perhaps, 'balance, roll and jump' (spin turn). The sequences are learned through repetition, and to become skilful at the 'hop, skip and jump', the components must be broken down into:

- hop : one-leg take-off, same-leg landing;

- skip: one-leg take-off, other-leg landing;

- jump: one-leg take-off, two-foot landing.

Motion sensitivity (Stein and Glickstein 1992) and problems with convergence have been identified in many children and adults with dyslexia: catching a ball can prove quite problematic. As described in Chapter 3, start by developing coordinated hand movements – to 'clap' bubbles. This encourages the child to stretch up, down and sideways, judging distances and speed of travel.

1. Move on from bubbles to paper balls (see Appendices). They are easier to control than balloons and come in a range of sizes. They can be caught, thrown and hit with a bat.

2. Progress with beanbags, sponge and Koosh balls before using tennis and basketballs. Ask the child to adopt a standing position and to watch the ball. Start with a two-handed catch and gradually increase the distance.

   Support: Make sure that the thrower is competent. Provide a rubber spot or hoop and encourage the child to stay close to it.

3. One-handed catch. Use a soft ball that is an appropriate size for the child. Repeat the activity until the skill is mastered.

   Support: Sometimes the other hand gets in the way. Many children master the task more quickly if they are holding something in the 'unused' hand.

4. Extend two-handed and one-handed catching to solid balls. Vary the distance from the thrower. Introduce a bounce before

the catch so that the child begins to work out the 'angle of deflection'.

Support: Try to use brightly coloured objects for catching. It helps children who have visual-processing problems.

5. Throwing – demonstrate using a large sponge ball held with both hands at chest height. Mark a target on the wall sufficiently large for the children to achieve success.

Support: Children with coordination difficulties often apply different pressure with each hand, causing the ball to spin. Provide assistance by placing your hand over theirs and 'throw' with them.

6. As two-handed competency using a large ball develops, develop one-handed skills.

    Start with a beanbag or something that is unlikely to roll away. Place large coloured discs or mats on the floor, ask the children to 'throw the frog onto the lily pad'. Use both hands separately.

Support: Start with short distances, with gradual increases. Again, you may observe a range of associated movements.

7. Extend the task using a small ball and basket. Figure 7.4 shows a child aiming an underarm throw with his right hand. His left arm and hand are also raised.

Figure 7.4

In the next picture (Figure 7.5), his attempt at an overarm shot is accompanied by a raised right leg.

He is given a baton to hold in his left hand and the shots are repeated, underarm (Figure 7.6) and overarm (Figure 7.7).

Immediately his balance and coordination improves. With the baton his success in ten attempts at throwing (five times each hand) was seven: without the baton he achieved only three.

Figure 7.5

Figure 7.6

Figure 7.7

8. Greater emphasis is placed on bat/ball skills as the child progresses through KS1 and KS2, then onto secondary education. The child learns to hold the bat (two hands) and to balance a beanbag on the top. That, perhaps, is not too difficult, until the additional dimension of walking forwards is included. After a great deal of trial and error, the Year 1 children master the skill (Figure 7.8).

Figure 7.8

9. When the child is able to balance a ball on the bat, an adult can hold the ball above the surface and drop it centrally, so that the child can hit it. Use a bat with a large surface area. Extend the activity, throwing the ball from a distance of one metre.

   Support: This will require a great deal of practice and it is easier to begin with paper balls.

10. Develop underarm action before attempting overarm. Involve children in team games such as 'rounders' and cricket.

    Support: Make sure that children who have difficulty catching and directing their throws do not have responsibility for bowling or standing at any of the bases: they could be held responsible for their team losing the game.

11. Kicking – establish that one-leg balance has been achieved. Encourage the child to kick the ball anywhere, using the specific parts of the foot – toe, outside and inside edges. Kick the ball against a wall and then mark a target or use a goal.

Support: Primary-aged pupils have wide-ranging skills depending largely on the amount of practice they have had. Some will have been kicking balls from the time they learned to walk; others will have had very little experience. It is important to extend the skills of all children in a class group so the tasks can be differentiated.

The target can be the size of a goal (Figure 7.9). Mark two-metre and four-metre lines and place a smaller target within the goal.

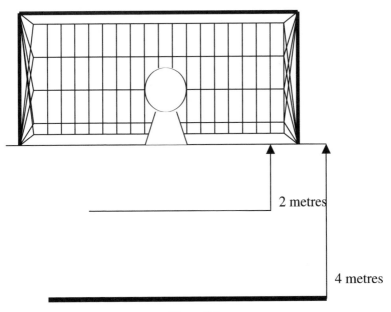

Figure 7.9

A point is gained for scoring a 'goal' in the net from the shortest distance. Increasing the distance and hitting the target can gain extra points.

Working in pairs and teams

12. Mirror images: direct the children to form two lines facing each other. Working in pairs, the children take it in turns to 'mirror' each other's movements. With young children, restrict it to head, then hand and arm movements. Extend the activity to include single-leg balance (Figure 7.10).

Figure 7.10

Support: The children could practise in the mirror first to give them an idea of the movements they could try.

13. The parachute is popular for pre-school children and teenagers alike. The activities can be varied to accommodate the ages and abilities of the children.

    Walking forwards, holding the parachute, and then turning the opposite way, encourages children to coordinate their movements to comply with the rest of the group.

Age-appropriate targets can be set, e.g., for pre-school and nursery children 'Keep the Teddy on the top'. Lifting the parachute high by selected pupils (all those holding a red segment for example), running underneath (Figure 7.11) and keeping two balls bouncing on the surface without falling off (Figure 7.12) are great fun for KS2 children.

Support: The activity is supportive of children who have difficulty responding quickly to moving objects. Each child holds part of the parachute, so if the approaching ball has to be directed back to the centre, hopefully the children on either side will react, raising their arms high. This models the required behaviour and the action can be repeated when the ball returns.

14. Collaborative games: the challenge (Figure 7.13) requires the child at one end of the bench to make their way to the other

Figure 7.11	Figure 7.12

Figure 7.13

without falling off. As is evident from the photos, the 'team' are providing mutual support, hanging onto each other as progress is made down the line.

Support: This is a very inclusive activity and all children, regardless of their physical skills have virtually the same chance of achievement.

15. Rhythm and movement is highlighted as another problem area for many children with dyslexia. Begin with a regular beat, with hands or, better still, a tambourine. Young children (Foundation Stage) can sit on the floor holding a ball above V-shaped legs. Give the instruction to bounce the ball after every three beats, e.g. 1-2-3 drop, 1-2-3 drop. Vary the timings – 1-drop, 1-drop – to develop listening skills and encourage the child to coordinate movement in response to sound.

Support: Many dyslexic children have great problems sequencing sounds, let alone trying to incorporate movement. 'Rebecca' always struggled when trying to join in with the nursery rhymes; she could never make the action fit the words. After several weeks of the activity described above, everything suddenly seemed to fit together. By the end of her time in nursery, her responses to rhythm and movement were the same as those of her peers.

16. Older pupils can engage in similar activities, perhaps standing or balancing on a low beam. Figures 7.14 and 7.15 are upper KS2 pupils attempting 1-2-3-bounce, 1-bounce, as a repeated sequence.

Figure 7.14   **Figure 7.15**

17. In the next exercise, still using the beat from a tambourine, the pupils pass the ball round in a circle. Figures 7.16–7.19 show the instructions: pass, pass, bounce, catch.

Figure 7.16

Figure 7.17

Figure 7.18

Figure 7.19

18. As the pupils become more skilled, introduce additional balls into the circle so several are being passed at the same time.

There are many schemes that offer structured PE activities for pupils. Select those that show evidence of progression in the targets set and take into account the problems experienced by many children with dyslexia and other specific learning difficulties. Break them down into smaller achievable steps. Make sure that the children have regular opportunities to practise new skills and those recently acquired.

Chapter 8

Developing Skills – Secondary Education

Physical Education through KS1 and KS2 lays the foundation for entry to secondary schooling. Children may already be aware of their relative strengths and weaknesses and there is a greater opportunity for those with coordination difficulties to choose activities in which they can excel. Strength and stamina are an integral part of the PE curriculum at this stage, so style can give way to sheer determination.

A survey of adults recently completed for a health club chain asked, 'What do you remember about PE in Senior school?' Top of the list was the 'cross-country run' (Figure 8.1).

Figure 8.1

It comes as a shock to most students: from running the odd 100 metres now and then, suddenly there is a requirement to run one, if not several, miles.

Building strength and stamina can be a target for all children, regardless of their physical competency. These form the basis of distance running and, with opportunities to develop these skills, youngsters who may find coordinated activities more challenging, can achieve as well as their peers.

Teenagers are very conscious of their self-image and those experiencing difficulties are better motivated to practise at home, away from the attentions of their peers. Activities that develop muscle strength and tone can be practised in a relatively limited space (Figures 8.2 and 8.3).

Figure 8.2   **Figure 8.3**

Balance skills extend, and this can be a collaborative exercise involving a number of pupils. Figure 8.4 shows four students of different abilities preparing to stand, with body leaning forward and one leg extended backwards. The pupils are directed to touch hands centrally and this provides support for those less able.

Together (Figure 8.5) the students achieve success. Individually, one of the students would have found the task very difficult.

Figure 8.6 illustrates balance skills in Year 7 pupils. The task becomes more complex and requires higher-level skills, as observed in a group of Year 9 pupils (Figure 8.7).

The progression of skills through KS1 and KS2 prepares pupils for the higher levels of competency required in secondary education. Learning the correct movements associated with jumping – for example: on the spot, over a line, over a bench, then 'small hurdles' – is excellent training for the high jump. (Figures 8.8 and 8.9).

Figure 8.4

Figure 8.5

Figure 8.6

Figure 8.7

'Kicking' skills improve greatly during KS3, with opportunities to become involved in more team games. Kicking progresses from the 'high leg kick' (Figure 8.10), typical of many Year 7 children, to the more controlled ball skills evident by Year 9. The group (Figure 8.11) are practising 'foot, knee, chest' techniques.

In Figures 8.12 and 8.13, Lee skilfully kicks from 'foot to head'. Figure 8.12 shows how the movement begins, balancing the ball on the foot. This illustrates the progression from Figure 5.8 when the child is learning to balance a beanbag on his extended foot.

Figure 8.8

Figure 8.9

Figure 8.10

Figure 8.11

These skills then transfer into the game (Figure 8.14). The Year 6 child is concentrating on shooting at goal, aiming at the target and running with the ball positioned on the ground. Figure 8.15 shows the Year 9 pupil controlling the ball with his chest. His body is stationary and he has much greater control and time to plan into which part of the net he will direct the ball.

In adolescence, youngsters go through a period of great physical change. Changes in weight distribution and balance occur during the 'growth spurt'. Changes in height can be of great advantage in netball and basketball (Figure 8.16), but the brain's calculations, which

Figure 8.12

Figure 8.13

Figure 8.14

Figure 8.15

plan the 'mechanics' of movement, i.e. the angle of the arm and hand, and the velocity of the throw to manoeuvre the ball through the hoop – must be reprogrammed.

Skills acquired in KS1 and KS2 require continuing practice through secondary schooling.

As mentioned previously, the Secondary PE curriculum allows for further development of movement skills and provides greater breadth of opportunity. Students have access to tennis, squash and badminton courts (Figure 8.17).

Track markings measure distances accurately, so improvements in speed can be recorded. Building on the development of basic throwing skills, new activities, such as discus and javelin, introduce new techniques.

Figure 8.16

Figure 8.17

Lunch and after-school clubs provide opportunities for practice. Many pupils who have difficulties acquiring motor skills have very low self-esteem. This becomes more evident on transfer to secondary school. It is important for these youngsters to focus their attention on the development of skills where there has been some evidence of success. Everyone, with practice, is capable of becoming competent in at least one skill area. Where problems exist, target particular skills early; if the pupil does not have a particular focus then there is the possibility that nothing will be achieved to a level of personal satisfaction.

If we refer back to the skills developed by the well-known sportspeople with dyslexia, it could point the direction for many youngsters with dyslexia who are undecided as to where their talents might lie.

Activities involving strength and stamina are high on the list: swimming, rowing, track and field events (Bruce Jenner, Olympic gold medallist, decathlon). These are generally skills that require good balance and motor development but, to a much lesser degree, a perceptual component. The skills are a constant repetition of similar movements: skills that can be practised repeatedly.

The focus is on the direct control of body movements, which generally are not influenced by external, uncontrolled factors, e.g. the movement of a ball or another team member.

The skills in which the majority of these notable sportspeople excel are those that are predictable, i.e. the individual is only required to set personal targets, e.g. improving speed or developing 'style', moving more fluently to maximise the effect.

Given that the time taken for many children with dyslexia to acquire 'new skills' follows the 'square root rule' (described in Chapter 3), and the constraints of the National Curriculum, much of the 'practice' will be external to the school environment.

These children would obviously benefit from accessing a programme of structured learning activities, where the focus is on the development of balance and motor skills. To support the learning difficulties associated with dyslexia, the movements should be described through demonstration. In addition, the tasks must be broken down into small, achievable personal targets, with opportunities for repetition and practice.

A solution is offered in the next chapter.

Chapter 9

Physical Education – Positive Solutions

Research confirms that many children and adults with dyslexia have problems with the development of motor skills. This has implications for learning, which include problems with handwriting, the speed of information processing and the likelihood of low self-esteem.

Discussion with numerous children and their parents suggests that, for some, the solution to the problem can be found within an organisation promoting the development of martial arts, and more specifically, Taekwondo. Case studies, which will be presented at the end of this chapter, illustrate the transformations that have occurred in children's lives; but first it is necessary to understand why this sport has produced such positive outcomes.

Taekwondo – development in the UK

Taekwondo is the national martial art of Korea. It became an accredited event in the 2000 Olympic Games and its origins can be traced back to ancient times.

The movements practised today were evidenced in wall paintings dating back to 57 BC; however, it was only after the Korean War (1950–53) that Taekwondo was promoted outside of Korea. There are now clubs in more than 100 countries, and in 1973 the World Taekwondo Federation (WTF) was established.

Taekwondo clubs in the UK are expected to adhere to the guidelines produced by the Federation. Master David Jordinson

(7th Dan) heads the Chungdokwan Taekwondo Organisation, affiliated to the British Taekwondo Control Board, and he invited me to meet with instructors, observe training classes and talk to students.

The sport appeals to individuals of all ages and abilities: it provides a totally inclusive environment where students aspire to achieve their personal targets. A number had learning difficulties, some had significant physical problems – 'Dawn', with mild cerebral palsy, and 'Susan', with chronic arthritis, was in a wheelchair.

Figure 9.1 Master David Jordinson and Master Steve Robinson

For the majority, there were no outward signs, but many had suffered at the hands of bullies because of their coordination difficulties, which were most evident in PE. Children who had become reluctant school attendees were described by their parents as having been 'transformed'. How had this happened?

The fundamental principle of Taekwondo is that everyone can achieve. Instructors are required to understand the physiology of physical development and the acquisition of motor skills. It is with this knowledge that achievable personal targets can be identified. As stated by the WTF, 'The purpose and objective of an Instructor is to support those individuals developing skills, to achieve.'

The instructors provide specified programmes of skill development and they select teaching methods most appropriate to the learning of stated objectives. Ultimately, problems with motor planning and coordination will be replaced by 'conditioned reflexes', which can be developed through repeated practice of basic movements.

The skills selected must be appropriate for the age and maturity of the student. The Organisation provides information defining the characteristics of development at particular ages and recommends the most appropriate corresponding methods of Taekwondo instruction.

Summary of information

Students aged 9 and under

Development

Coordination is immature and there may be some visual instability. Posture is not erect and motor skill development is undisciplined and comprises mainly running, jumping and climbing. Perceptual skills are developing and children struggle to reach targets correctly.

They can be directed to work in groups of three or four and, while they enjoy team games, the rules must be simple and not competitive. Movement activities should not exceed 30 minutes.

Children of this age can be easily disturbed, and the instructor should be sensitive to voice tone.

Visual perceptual skills and motion sensitivity is developing, which brings greater awareness of distance, speed and position in space.

Method of instruction

- Children at this stage of development enjoy working in groups, so firm boundaries should be established.

- The children must learn to respond to the direction of the instructor.

- Training at this stage is directed towards improving the children's spontaneous physical development. Expect progress, not perfection.

- Emphasis is placed on developing basic movement skills by teaching whole-body movements, balance, arm positions, leg kicks and patterns, which enhance coordination skills.

- This stage of development is viewed as an educational period of body movements rather than training techniques.

- Students are encouraged to work with a partner, even during warming-up exercises.

Pupils aged 10–13

Youngsters of this age have more stamina, with height and weight increasing steadily. They continue to enjoy activities such as running and chasing one another, and they become more competitive.

Posture is still relatively weak, but accelerated learning is evident in the acquisition of basic movement and coordination skills.

Response to adult direction is variable and they respond more openly to peer instruction. Pupils of this age become more self-conscious and are aware if they have any difficulty acquiring skills.

Ability to remember sequences improves and it becomes easier to learn movement patterns.

Method of instruction

- There is emphasis on the development and extension of motor skills.

- To improve techniques, instructions are broken down and movement patterns are practical.

- Building physical strength is part of the focus of development.

- It is more evident, at this stage, when students experience difficulty developing 'new skills'. Particular attention must be given to these individuals and incentives provided to raise self-confidence and a willingness to continue to try and master the skill.

Pupils aged 14–16

Development

- A growth spurt in height and weight is evident. Greater control over breathing and its effect on strength should be the focus of attention.

- Commitment to developing skills with higher levels of stamina, to train for longer periods.

- Greater ability to question and correct mistakes and so improve skills.

Method of instruction

- Verbal explanations support demonstration of techniques.

- Students just beginning the sport show great variations in physical ability. Those with difficulty developing motor skills are more obvious in this group: they must receive individual support and encouragement immediately as they will make comparisons between themselves and their more able peers.

- Skills must still be acquired in stages and progression is evident if appropriate targets are set.

The process of learning techniques is divided into three stages:

1. *Perceptual.* The student 'plans' the physical movements they are to undertake: their success is dependent upon previous learning experiences. The instructor is able to judge the student's level of competence and gives sufficient information to progress the skill.

2. *Fixation.* When attempting to execute a 'new skill' there are many errors. With practice, the student reformulates the 'planning' of the activity and, through a process of constant repetition, the errors begin to decrease.

3. *Automatisation.* With sufficient repetition, automatisation or 'automaticity' (Fawcett and Nicolson 1996) is achieved. The technique is performed without having to make any perceptual adjustment.

In previous chapters the most successful teaching methods to encourage the development of physical skills in pupils with specific learning difficulties have highlighted the need for:

- Demonstration

- Correction

- Repetition

- Setting personal targets

- Maturation.

The model for the development of skills in Taekwondo encompasses all of these recommendations. In addition, each skill is broken down into its basic components. The next section examines these basic movements and illustrates how they combine to form the sequences that characterise the sport. When basic skills are secure, the student is given instruction to master more complex, coordinated techniques.

Hand positions

Figure 9.2 illustrates the hand positions 1, 2 and 3 which form a fist. Fisted hands can be presented turning forwards or backwards in 'attack' and 'defence' positions. When the hand is open, the four fingers are extended, side by side, while keeping their last joints turned slightly inwards (Figure 9.3).

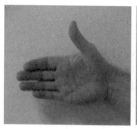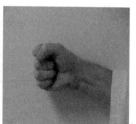

Figure 9.2

Figure 9.3

The thumb is held slightly crooked at the first joint, turning towards the forefinger.

Foot positions

The positions of the legs and feet are fundamental to the balance of the body when standing, turning, lowering, stretching, jumping and kicking.

In Taekwondo, it is recognised that foot techniques are less flexible and accurate than hand movements so they must have greater focus during training. It is important to learn how the balance of the body changes when one foot is raised, and forward and backward movement is introduced in activities such as jumping and kicking. The student learns to balance with legs slightly apart, both feet facing forwards, with soles flat on the floor. Next, the 'ready' stance is adopted (Figure 9.4), left foot forwards, right foot back, turned at an angle of 90 degrees.

Figure 9.4 Master Russell Shaw

When raised from the floor, the upper surface, the side or the ball of the foot form a range of different techniques.

Figure 9.5 illustrates the front kick (1st and 2nd positions) and back kick. Note the foot is extended, and then pulled back.

Figure 9.6 is a demonstration of first position side kick, when the edge (blade) of the foot extends towards the opponent (Figure 9.7).

Figure 9.5

Figure 9.6   **Figure 9.7**

Balance and movement are gradually combined with these basic skills to develop the student's motor sensitivity and coordination.

The pictures which follow are those of KS1 and KS2 pupils who are demonstrating a range of newly acquired techniques. Alongside them are references to activities in previous chapters developing similar skills. In a single chapter it is impossible to include every movement, but a selection has been made from those that align very closely with the physical skills expected in children, primarily of primary, but also secondary age.

Warming up – stretching exercises

(The figures in brackets refer to the movements described in previous chapters.)

When engaging in physical exercise, it is important to warm up and wind down at the beginning and end of the lesson. The pictures illustrating 'splits' show students who are developing their skills, both using arms and hands to provide additional support. Children should not be asked to move into these positions until they have worked up to this level of competence.

Coordinated balance

These activities are progressive: the first sequence in Taekwondo combining hands, feet and balance is at the beginning of the preliminary pattern (*poomsae*) of movements, necessary for

**One leg balance, high rising knee
(Figure 5.11)**

**Long forward stance
(Figure 4.7)**

Front splits (Figure 5.23)

Box splits (Figure 5.24)

students to pass their first grading. This is a 'back stance, double guard and block'. The 'crane stance' at the end of the illustrations in this section is part of a black belt (master grade) *poomsae* 'Keumgang'.

The basic movements are described by the WTF as the 'preliminary actions towards the *poomsae*, which is made up of a series of offensive and defensive techniques'.

As the student improves his/her skills the patterns become more demanding, but can be mastered 'through repeated practice of each separate basic movement'.

Other elements of the training include self-defence – moves to protect while preventing an attack – and sparring – the culmination of all the practised skills, attack and defence with self-control.

Back stance, double guard and block

Back stance, X-fist block

Sitting stance: obverse punch
(Figure 5.19)

Sitting stance, inner and outer block
(Figure 5.4)

Forward crane stance:
high rise block and low block
(Figures 5.6 and 6.3)

Backward crane stance: foot behind
knee and spear fingered strike

The next series of photographs shows students from KS1 displaying such controlled movements.

Front kick (Figures 5.8 and 8.12)

Side kick (Figure 8.5)

Low section reverse turning kick
(Figures 5.22 and 5.23)

Two high-rising blocks and two low
blocks (Figure 7.10)

In the next sequence, two KS2 pupils, both black belts, demonstrate sparring.

Hook kick

Side kick (Figure 8.5)

In the next two photographs, the girl is reacting to a 'long forward stance, obverse punch' attack.

Sitting stance 'C'-shaped block (Figures 4.5 and 4.6)

Outer block, side-kick to mid-section (Figure 5.9 and 5.10)

This final illustration is a KS3 black belt (2nd Dan) student demonstrating a 'flying side kick', which involves controlled running, jumping, balance and coordinated movement. (See Figures 6.14 and 8.9).

Students of all ages study Taekwondo. Some move more quickly through the grades than others, and all students, in consultation with the instructor, decide their personal targets. The skills are acquired in small steps and repeated opportunities to practise allows for automatisation. The students know exactly what will be required from them at their grading and they can be examined when they are competent in their skill development.

There are eight Kup grades, reducing in number, before achieving a black belt. Students then go on to higher Dan grades.

The progression is as follows:

	Coloured belt	Grade
Junior black belt students	White	New
	Yellow	8th Kup
	Yellow & Green tag	7th Kup
	Green	6th Kup
	Green & Blue tag	5th Kup
	Blue	4th Kup
	Blue & Red Tag	3rd Kup
	Red	2nd Kup
	Red & Black Tag	1st Kup
	Black belt	1st Dan
		2nd Dan
		3rd Dan
	Master grades	4th Dan
		5th Dan
		6th Dan
		7th Dan

Master David Jordinson (7th Dan) believes that many students attend classes to improve their physical skills in a positive environment. The focus is not only on motor skills, but also on developing fitness and stamina: many who enter the sport with diagnosed breathing difficulties, such as asthma, discover that by developing their techniques their need for medication and inhalers reduces significantly.

Students are taught through demonstration by instructors and paired with pupils of higher grades, so that movement skills are repeatedly modelled. The classes are extremely well disciplined and the students show respect towards each other as well as to the Master. When students know the boundaries, they can feel secure.

Case studies:

Luke, age 7

Luke was born three weeks prematurely and presented as a 'sickly' child throughout his first year. He had problems chewing solid food and his diet was quite restricted. He had developed a single-word vocabulary prior to nursery entry but his language was immature. He avoided jigsaw puzzles and inset boards and he showed no interest in looking at books.

At nursery, his mother described him as a child who had no interest in learning. 'He just wanted to play.' Six months after entry into full-time education, it was acknowledged that Luke had specific learning difficulties. He was diagnosed with dyslexia and, despite having had private tuition for a year, he achieved only Level 1 in his SAT in English, compared with Level 2b in Maths.

He had no confidence in his school work and no confidence in himself: he needed time to process information and to respond. He was easily distracted and disliked school.

Luke loves Taekwondo: 'it is something for him to achieve'. He attends three lessons every week, which enables him to spend extra time learning his moves. Through repetition, he is able to remember his patterns. He has a blue belt and is determined to continue to black and beyond. He never has to be reminded to go, unlike other activities. Luke is 'thrilled' every time he moves to the next grade and there are targets he can achieve every few months.

Jamie, age 8

Jamie started Taekwondo when he was aged 5. He has recently graded to black tag and is currently training for black belt. There is a family history of dyslexia and, when in Year 1, Jamie had problems with concentration and continued to reverse letters, he was referred for assessment. Initially, Jamie wrote with his left hand, and then he switched to his right. His difficulties have been the cause of some aggressive behaviour. Despite a range of interventions, problems persist with concentration. Jamie has a Statement of Special Education Needs that highlights specific difficulties in language and literacy. Jamie also attends three sessions of Taekwondo each week, and besides progressing through the grades, he has also achieved success in a number of competitions. His mother questions how he can remain focused and on task for 90 minutes in Taekwondo and yet is unable to manage more than a few minutes elsewhere.

The answer has to be in the strategy:

- Achievable personal targets

- Opportunities for repetition

- High levels of support

- Rewards that are tangible

- Motivation to achieve

Sammy, age 10

Sammy had always been a very anxious child who found it difficult to mix with her peers. She was told she was dyslexic when she was eight. She also had problems with perception and coordination. She was last to be picked for team games, the usual PE activity, both indoors and outdoors, and was usually held responsible for her team losing. This was far more concerning to her than her reading difficulties.

For the first two weeks of attending Taekwondo, she sat with a parent at the back of the hall. She watched the 'warm-up' activities and practised them at home. She became more involved in the weeks that followed, joining in with some activities, sitting out for others. No-one ever questioned why, probably because many other joining children had behaved similarly. Eventually she developed the confidence to join in with everything. She was awarded a prize for 'Student of the month', because for her to participate fully in class was a far greater achievement than obtaining high marks in the grading. Her parents believed that this was the turning point. Sammy went on to grade every four months and, shortly, she will be examined for 2nd Kup.

Her increasing confidence has translated into improved attainments in school. Although reading and spelling difficulties had been identified by parents and school staff as the major problem, this was not the case for Sammy. Her secondary difficulties were the main barrier to learning.

Sometimes it can be difficult to prevent a cycle of school failure where the child constantly focuses on apparently unattainable targets, often set by themselves. Raising self-esteem in an alternative setting can produce positive benefits in school and at home.

Chapter 10

Conclusion

Research confirms that the majority of children with dyslexia experience problems with the development of motor skills, which do not disappear with maturation. Delays in motor development are usually associated with deficits in perceptual skills and difficulties with the speed of (visual/auditory) information processing.

By identifying these specific, rather than generalised, difficulties in the acquisition of physical skills and by providing structured activities to develop them, learning outcomes improve. Myers (2002) reported on a small-scale study involving 20 KS1 pupils. All were identified as having problems with language and literacy and some had not developed any reading skills. Half of the pupils arrived early for school and spent ten minutes each day working on a structured programme to develop balance and motor skills. A term later, the pupils were reassessed. There were significant differences between the two groups in their development of reading skills, perceptual ability and concentration.

There are increasing numbers of young children identified with coordination difficulties. For some, it is merely lack of opportunity, for others the skills have not been acquired 'naturally' so they need to be broken down into smaller, structured steps.

Children with dyslexia require repeated opportunities to practise 'new skills' and develop automaticity, especially when more than one operation is involved, e.g. balancing on a beam or catching a ball. Activities which are of greatest benefit concentrate initially on balance, then motor, then coordination skills. Posture must be secured (Kohen-Raz 1986; Fawcett and Nicolson 1999) before competency can be achieved in other areas.

The fundamental elements of 'best practice' to develop physical skills are:

- tasks must be broken down into small steps;

- only personal targets should be set;

- targets must be achievable and show progression;

- skills must be demonstrated; and

- repeated opportunities to learn.

This structure will help all children struggling to develop physical skills, not just those identified with dyslexia.

> Attention, balance and coordination are fundamental for learning. In view of these facts, opportunities for movement and physical education are as important as the teaching of literacy and maths, especially in the early learning years. (Goddard-Blyth 2000)

Appendix:
Useful Addresses

British Dyslexia Association
98 London Road
Reading RG1 5AU
Tel: (helpline) 0118 966 8271
Tel: (administration) 0118 966 2677
Fax: 0118 935 1927
e-mail: admin@bda-dyslexia.demon.co.uk
Website: http://www.bda-dyslexia.org.uk/

The Dyspraxia Foundation
8 West Alley
Hitchin
Herts SG5 1EG
Tel: (helpline) 01462 454986
Tel: (administration) 01462 455016
Fax: 01462 455052
e-mail:admin@dyspraxiafoundation.org.uk
Website: http://www.dyspraxiafoundation.org.uk

Tumble Tots
Blue Bird Park
Bromsgrove Road
Hunnington
Halesowen
West Midlands
B62 0JW
Tel: 0121 585 7003

Chungdokwon Taekwondo
Master Steve Robinson
Ferryhill Leisure Centre
Lambton Road
Ferryhill
Co. Durham
DL17 8BQ
Tel: 01388 720415
e-mail: ferryhill@chungdo.org
Website: http://chungdo.org

Youth Sport Trust
Loughborough University
Loughborough
Leics LE11 3TU
Tel: 01509 263171

Davies – The Sports People
Novara House
Ashby Park
Asby de la Zouch
Leics LE65 1NG
Tel: 0115 945 2203

Plus Balls
79 Victoria Road
Cirencester
Gloucs GL7 1ES
Tel: 01285 659133

References and Further Reading

Beaton, A. A. (2002) 'Dyslexia and the cerebellar deficit hypothesis', *Cortex*, **38**, 479–90.

Denckla, M. B. (1985) 'Motor co-ordination in dyslexic children: theoretical and clinical implications', in F. H. Duffy and N. Geschwind (eds), *Dyslexia: A Neuroscientific Approach to Clinical Evaluation.* Boston, MA: Little Brown, pp. 182–205.

Denckla, M. B., Rudel, R. G., Chapman, C. and Kreiger, J. (1985) 'Motor proficiency in dyslexic children with and without attentional disorders'. *Arch Neurol,* **42**(3), 228–31.

Duffy, F. H. and Geschwind, N. (eds) (1985) *Dyslexia: A Neuroscientific Approach to Clinical Evaluation.* Boston, MA: Little Brown.

Eden, G. F. *et al.* (1996) *Abnormal Processing of Visual Motion in Dyslexia Revealed by Functional Brain Imaging.*

Fawcett, A. J. (2001) 'Dyslexia and the cerebellum'. *Patoss Bulletin*, November, 2–5.

Fawcett, A. J. and Nicolson, R. I. (1992) 'Automatisation deficits in balance or dyslexic children'. *Perceptual and Motor Skills,* **75**, 507–29.

Fawcett, A. J. and Nicolson, R. I. (1995) 'Persistent deficits in motor skill of children with dyslexia'. *Journal of Motor Behaviour,* **27**(3), 235–40.

Fawcett, A. J. and Nicolson, R. I. (1996) *The Dyslexia Screening Test.* London: The Psychological Corporation.

Fawcett, A. J. and Nicolson, R. I. (1999) 'Performance of dyslexic children on cerebellar and cognitive tests'. *Journal of Motor Behaviour,* **31**, 68–78.

Fawcett, A. J., Nicolson, R. I. and Dean, P. (1996) 'Impaired performance of children with dyslexia on a range of cerebellar tasks'. *Annals of Dyslexia,* **46**, 259–83.

Fawcett, A. J., Nicolson, R. I. and MacLagan, F. (2001) 'Cerebellar tests may differentiate between poor readers with and without IQ discrepancy'. *Journal of Learning Disabilities,* **24**(2), 119–35.

Finch, A. J., Nicolson, R. I. and Fawcett, A. J. (2002) 'Evidence for a neuroanatomical difference within the olivo-cerebellar pathway of adults with dyslexia'. *Cortex*, **38**, 529–39.

Frederickson, N., Frith, U. and Reason, R. (1997) *Phonological Assessment Battery*. Windsor: NFER-NELSON.

Goddard-Blyth, S. A. (1995) 'The role of reflexes in the development of the visual system'. *Journal of Behavioural Optometry*, **6**(2), 31–5.

Goddard-Blyth, S. A. and Hyland, D. (1998) 'Screening for neurophysiological dysfunction in the specific learning difficulty child'. *British Journal of Occupational Therapy*, **61**, (10), 459–64.

Goddard-Blyth, S. A. (2000) 'Early learning in the balance: priming the fast ABC'. *Support for Learning*, **15**(4), 154–7.

Jordan, I. (2002) *Visual Dyslexia*. London: Jessica Kingsley.

Kaplan, B. J., Wilson, B. N., Dewey, D. and Crawford, S. G. (1998) 'DCD may not be a discrete disorder'. *Human Movement Science*, **17**, 471–90.

Kiphard, E. J. and Schilling, F. (1974) *The Body Coordination Test* (Beltz Test Gmbh). Germany: Weinhem.

Kohen-Raz, R. (1986) *Learning Disabilities and Postural Control*. London: Freund.

Livingstone, M. S. *et al.* (1991) 'Physiological and anatomical evidence for a magnocellular defect in developmental dyslexia'. *Proceedings of the National Academy of Sciences USA*, **88**, 7943–7.

Mcdonald, J. and McCann, J. (1991) *Primary Physical Education in County Durham*. Durham LEA.

McCrory, E., Frith, U., Brunswick, N. and Price, C. (2000) 'Abnormal functional activation during a simple word repetition task: a PET study of adult dyslexics'. *Journal Cognitive Neuroscience*, **12**(5), 753–62.

Myers, S. (2002) 'Assessing the effects of a daily structured motor-skills programme on the attainments, concentration and self-esteem in group of Key Stage 1 pupils'. Special Study, University of Durham.

Nicolson, R. I. and Fawcett, A. J. (1990) 'Automaticity: a new framework for dyslexic research?' *Cognition*, **35**(2), 159–82.

Nicolson, R. I. and Fawcett, A. J. (1994) 'Reaction times and dyslexia'. *Quarterly Journal Experimental Psychology* [A], **47**(1), 29–48.

Nicolson, R. I., Fawcett, A. J., *et al.* (1999) 'Association of abnormal cerebellar activation with motor learning difficulties in dyslexic adults'. *Lancet*, **353**(9165), 1662–7.

Nicolson, R. I., Fawcett, A. J. and Dean, P. (2001) 'Dyslexia, development and the cerebellum'. *Trends Neuroscience*, **24**(9), 515–16.

Portwood, M. M. (1999) *Developmental Dyspraxia: Identification and Intervention: A Manual for Parents and Professionals* (2nd edn). London: David Fulton.

Portwood, M. M. (2000) *Understanding Developmental Dyspraxia: A Textbook for Students and Professionals*. London: David Fulton.

Ramus, F., Pidgeon, E. and Frith, U. (2003) 'The relationship between motor control and phonology in dyslexic children'. *Journal of Child Psychology and Psychiatry and Allied Disciplines*, **44** (in press).

Rudel, R. G. (1985) 'The definition of dyslexia: language and motor deficits,' in F. H. Duffy and N. Geschwind (eds), *Dyslexia: A Neuroscientific Approach to Clinical Evaluation*. Boston, MA: Little Brown, pp. 33–53.

Steffert, B. (1999) *Visual Spatial Ability and Dyslexia* (ed. Ian Padgett) London: St. Martin's College.

Stein, J. (2001) 'The magnocellular theory of developmental dyslexia'. *Dyslexia*, **7**, 12–36.

Stein, J. (2002) *The Magnocellular Theory in Relation to Dyslexia, Dyspraxia and ADHD*. Durham Conference.

Stein, J. F. and Glickstein, M. (1992) 'Role of the cerebellum in visual guidance of movement'. *Physiological Review*, **72**, 972–1017.

Stein, J. F. and Walsh, V. (1997) 'To see but not to read: the magnocellular theory of dyslexia'. *Trends in Neuroscience*, **20**, 147–53.

Un-youg, K. (1995) *Taekwondo Textbook*. Seoul: Oh-Sung.

Wetton, P. (1997) *Physical Education in the Early Years*. London: Routledge.

Willows, D. M., Kruk, R. S. and Corcos, E. (1993) 'Are there differences between disabled and normal readers in their processing of visual information'?, in Willows, D. M., Kruk, R. S. and Corcos, E. (eds), *Visual Processes in Reading and Reading Disabilities*. Hillsdale, NJ: Lawrence Erlbaum.

Wimmer, H., Mayringer, H. and Landerl, K. (1998) 'Poor reading: a deficit in skill-automatization or a phonological deficit?' *Scientific Studies of Reading*, **2**(4), 321–40.

Wolff, P. H. (1999) 'A candidate phenotype for familial dyslexia'. *European Child and Adolescent Psychiatry*, **8**(7), S021–S027.

Wolff, P. H., Cohen, C. and Drake, C. (1984) 'Impaired motor timing control in specific reading retardation'. *Neuropsychologica*, **22**(5), 587–600.

Wolff, P. H., Michel, G. F. and Ovrut, M. (1990) 'Rate and timing precision of motor coordination in developmental dyslexia'. *Developmental Psychology*, **26**, 349–59.

Index